Living Well
with
Bad Credit

Living Well
with
Bad Credit

Buy a House,
Start a Business,
 and Even
Take a Vacation–
  No Matter How Low
  Your Credit Score Is

CHRIS BALISH & GEOFF WILLIAMS

Health Communications, Inc.
Deerfield Beach, Florida

www.hcibooks.com

Library of Congress Cataloging-in-Publication Data

Balish, Chris.
    Living well with bad credit : buy a house, start a business, and even take a
vacation—no matter how low your credit score is / Chris Balish and Geoff Williams.
        p. cm.
    Includes index.
    ISBN-13: 978-0-7573-1358-5
    ISBN-10: 0-7573-1358-2
    1. Consumer credit—United States.   2. Commercial credit—United States.
3. Credit scoring systems—United States.   4. Finance, Personal—United States.
I. Williams, Geoffrey, 1970-   II. Title.
HG3756.U54B35 2010
332.024—dc22

                                                                    2009044834

©2010 Chris Balish and Geoff Williams

Publisher: Health Communications, Inc.
            3201 S.W. 15th Street
            Deerfield Beach, FL 33442–8190

Cover design by Larissa Hise Henoch
Interior design and formatting by Lawna Patterson Oldfield

CONTENTS

INTRODUCTION: BAD CREDIT HAPPENS TO GOOD PEOPLE

SIFT THROUGH THE RUBBLE THAT was once your house after a tornado storms your community, and you're probably not going to hear anyone whisper, "Well, he had it coming to him." Nobody sees someone lying in a hospital bed and thinks, "She must be a bad person." And these days there is little stigma attached to being divorced.

But the moment you hear someone has bad credit . . .

Fortunately, the negative stereotypes and assumptions associated with people who have bad credit are rapidly changing. Unfortunately, it took something like a giant gut-punch to the economy—often called the Great Recession—to change this stereotype. It's a shame the stereotype ever started in the first place, because while certainly there are plenty of deadbeats trying to game the system, it's never been a given that just because you have bad credit, you can't also be a good person.

Obviously, the stereotype quickly began fading after September 15, 2008, the day Lehman Brothers, a New York City–based international powerhouse financial services firm, failed. The collapse of

Lehman set off a panic throughout Wall Street, Main Street, Sesame Street, and every other street in the world, leading everyone to wonder if the foundation of the global economy just *appeared* to be constructed out of Scotch tape, chewing gum, and chicken wire.

Now, it seems, everyone either has bad credit or is about to. It's a trend. Hey, that's one positive thing about being deep in debt: you're trendy! Sorry . . . we don't mean to make light of a serious topic, but sometimes, when you're mired in debt, you almost have to. It's a shame that such a negative image of people with bad credit ever persisted in the first place, because while lots of people deserve their low credit scores, bad credit is also a result of good people having life come crashing down on them in an uncontrollable or unforeseen way. Think: divorce, disaster, a serious medical condition, or getting laid off from a job, not to mention the millions of people who slowly watch their credit card balances creep up, up, up over time, until they find themselves in too deep to dig out.

Fun fact: a perfect credit score is 850. **Not-so-fun fact:** the worst possible credit score is 300.

In other words, bad credit happens to the best of us. It is a fact and a sign of the times we live in that now more than ever, bad credit is happening to good people.

So cheer up! If you're feeling down about your finances and your FICO score, it's time to stop that. You are not alone; in fact, you're one of tens of millions in a similar situation. There is no shame in having a credit score that needs improvement. Dust yourself off, chin up, shoulders back, and stop being afraid of living with bad credit. The truth that the banks and credit card agencies don't want

you to know is that you can
live an awesome, fun, fulfilling
life with a very low credit score.

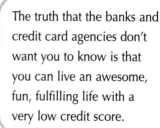

The truth that the banks and credit card agencies don't want you to know is that you can live an awesome, fun, fulfilling life with a very low credit score.

Don't worry—we're not living on another planet or pitching a lifestyle where one tries to have a bad credit score. This isn't a book where you'll find chapters like, "How to Buy a Mansion With No Money Down—in 17 Easy Steps." (We wish we were that smart.) No, think of this book as a how-to guide for people who like to live well no matter what. It's an instruction manual, with a mix of insight, anecdotes, pragmatic advice, and a dash of psychology—all designed to generate ideas to help you get through a tricky time with a little style.

But back to our earlier point, before we so rudely interrupted ourselves . . .

Banks and credit card companies don't want you to know that you can still live a wonderful life with a lousy credit history. The industry doesn't want you to know that it is still possible to purchase or lease a car, get a loan, buy a house, or rent an apartment—even if your credit score has been shattered.

It may sound kind of harsh to say that banks don't want people to know this information, but if you think about it, banks and credit card companies have a vested interest in making you petrified of your credit score; otherwise you might not be as keen to repay them. This partially explains why, in 2007, the credit bureau Experian released a report that many subprime mortgage borrowers were— think about this—paying their credit card bills *before* worrying about making their mortgage payments. The report surmised that these individuals wanted to keep their credit lines open, prevent their interest rates from rising due to a late payment, and protect their credit scores.

We get that. But isn't it sort of a warped strategy of prioritizing? Your home, whether a house or a rent payment, should always come first. Utilities next. Probably your car after that. The importance of buying food goes without saying, and medical care, especially for your kids, is right up there with your mortgage. Your credit card payment is important—we're not saying you shouldn't pay it—but in the big picture, it's probably the sixth or seventh most important bill that you have, not the first.

Having a bad credit score can cause problems and hassles. People are right to not want it and to do whatever they can to not get it. But *fear* of bad credit makes us do stupid things. (No offense—you'll learn soon how both of this book's two authors, and especially one of them, have made a lot of stupid errors when it comes to credit and debt.) Fear of bad credit makes us compound our mistakes, similar to the way that interest is compounded. Fear of bad credit even makes us desperate enough to seek out more credit. We believe that once you can let that fear go and accept your bad credit score, you may be on the path to eventually getting good credit.

But for first-timers and newcomers to the bad credit club, we know it's hard to accept being a member. Kenny Golde, who knows something about bad credit, is an independent filmmaker and the author of a book with a really long title—*The Do-It-Yourself Bailout: How I Reduced My Credit Card debt from $212,000 to $30,000 in Six Months and Saved over $100,000.* He got into a ton of debt after his business partner died. Kenny describes how he was able to settle his debts, which was a huge relief for him. But the downside was that he saw his credit score plummet 200 points.

As he told us, "What I would like to contribute to your book is the earth-shattering notion that one's credit score is *not* a reflection of who that person is as a person. We are (quite sadly) programmed to be 'proud' of our high credit scores, and conversely, to think less of others or ourselves if they (we) have poor credit scores. A terrible (and terribly common) occurrence these days is that someone with a once high credit score has it fall and then suffers a painful identity crisis in its wake."

If you're nodding your head right now because you sometimes confuse your self-worth with your actual worth, heed Golde's warning: "You are not your finances, and your credit score is not a reflection of who you are as a person. It's just a number. So if you have a low credit score right now, for whatever reason, yes, you must face the tangible reality of that in the form of higher interest on a loan, if you're looking for a loan right now, but you can freely abandon any guilt, shame, remorse, pain, fear, anxiety, or loss of identity that came with the reduced credit score; they are not connected."

Get that? You are *not* your credit score.

Joe Nicassio, a marketing guru who makes an appearance later in this book and who has dealt with his own share of bad credit, also has an interesting observation on FICO scores, which is the most common type of credit score: "If you think about it, banks have a vested interest in giving people low credit scores, because then it gives the bank a license to run your interest rate at 18 percent. If we're going to fix one thing in this country, we need to find a better way to judge people's characters than just a number on paper."

Whether you find the idea of a credit score abhorrent or perfectly reasonable, what goes onto your credit report stays there for at least seven years, and in some cases, a full decade; in the meantime, you have to live your life. So why not live the very best life you can right now? This book is all about helping you coexist with your bad credit score as peacefully, wisely, and happily as you can.

So pull up a chair. You're going to be in the Land of Bad Credit (LBC) for a while, so you might as well get comfortable. We're about to tell you how to make the best of a bad situation.

You are not your credit score.

CHAPTER ONE

WELCOME TO THE LAND OF BAD CREDIT

It is a strange thing that the man
who pays cash for all he gets cannot get credit
while a man who runs bills habitually can
get about all the credit he wants.

COMMENT MADE IN THE *WORTH COUNTY INDEX*,
JANUARY 3, 1907

IT ISN'T JUST THIS GENERATION that has been saddled by debt. Your grandparents had their own recessions and challenges in making payments to credit card companies and department stores. Back then it was Montgomery Ward and Sears; now it's Walmart and Amazon.com. Even your grandparents' grandparents struggled with money. If you've ever watched the 1970s TV show *Little House on the Prairie,* that series occasionally mangled the historical truth, but they were right on the money when they suggested that Charles Ingalls would have gotten credit at the mercantile store that Harriet and Nels Oleson owned.

We know you're anxious about the future, and maybe not all that interested in the past, but it helps to know how you got here. If you don't know what mistakes were made along the way, you can't fix them.

And as it turns out, credit problems have been brewing for a long time. Of course, for a long time everything worked pretty well, so we're not saying that every decision involving credit and debt for the last century has been built on a foundation of deceit and doom. Credit has a long and honorable history of working well. And yet, it's understandable why you got into debt in the first place. We have a rich history of spending money we don't have.

Even before the first national credit card—the Diner's Card—came along in 1949, there were credit cards issued by your local friendly neighborhood department store. These started getting popular in the 1930s, during the Great Depression. Nobody had money, and businesses were desperate to at least have the promise of future income. Before that, individual stores would routinely offer credit to their regular customers.

In fact, one of the first, and maybe *the* first, credit bureau actually showed up in Brooklyn around 1869, and by the 1890s credit bureaus were pretty commonplace throughout America. In fact, one of those 1890s bureaus, the Retail Credit Company, eventually became Equifax, which is one of the three giant credit agencies today.

The three major credit bureaus are Equifax, TransUnion, and Experian.

And what's so unsettling about debt history is how familiar everything is. The numbers get higher, but everything else pretty much stays the same. For instance, in

1896 the *New York Times* ran a detailed story about a lawyer who was having money problems (apparently they never divulged his name, to spare him any embarrassment). Anyway, one morning at breakfast, the attorney's wife handed him a bill for $5. He looked it over and said that the bill was "a small matter and the man could wait." Then the wife handed her husband a bill for $200. The lawyer again examined the bill, this time for a longer time. He finally handed it back, saying that the bill "was a large matter, and the man would have to wait."

See? Nothing changes. Human nature is human nature.

Consider the home equity loan, which seems like a pretty modern way of going into debt, due to its surge in popularity since the 1980s. But they've been around since at least the days of the Great Depression. Back in 1961, a Florida bank, St. Pete Federal, ran a newspaper ad explaining the home equity loan concept to their customers. "Chances are, you can get more money out of your home than you've put into it," the bank's ad read, adding that customers could use a home equity loan to "turn a weekend at the beach into a month in Europe. Turn a ski boat into a yacht." The advertisement's headline gushed, "It's like magic."

Like magic. No wonder so many of us are in trouble.

Not that we want to pass the buck (okay, maybe the wrong expression to use). Obviously, ultimately, we as individuals are the ones responsible for our money mismanagement. We signed on the dotted lines. Nobody forced us to get credit cards or take out loans. We have to own our mistakes, and boy, do we own them. But if you're going to beat yourself up, don't think for a second that you got into this all on your own. Banks have been holding your hand and whispering sweet nothings into your ear for quite some time now.

But let's talk about you. How'd you get here?

We don't know your situation, and won't know your situation, no matter how much you shout at this book. Still, we can almost guess. It seems like there are several paths to bad credit, and that most of us wind up on one of them, or a combination. We'll run through a few, and you can see if any of these sound familiar. Then we'll tell you a little about us, because while we both have a lot of empathy for what you're going through, one of us has actually gone through it.

You've Been Through a Divorce

This is a fairly common way to find yourself in bad credit territory, unfortunately. It's a weird, demoralizing outcome that adds insult to injury. You've just had your heart stomped on, and now your bank is kicking you when you're down. And bankers wear hard leather dress shoes.

No one enjoys going through a divorce, but when it happens, two people (or at least one of the two) are trying to improve their lives by moving on. Of course, you're not just breaking up a marriage; you're also breaking apart credit card debt, loans, finances, a mortgage, and your annual income.

Part of what goes wrong is that even if the court says that Mr. So-and-So is responsible for paying off the Visa card, it doesn't always work out that way. If the credit card was in both married couple's names, your credit issuer doesn't care what the court says. If it isn't paid off, Mrs. So-and-So gets a ding on her credit score as well. Or maybe the husband lets the wife and kids stay in the house, but because he can't afford to keep up with his new rent and new bills, he doesn't pay all of the child support he needs to pay, and so the wife can't make the mortgage payment, and the house goes into foreclosure, destroying two credit histories in the process. Well, as you can see, the scenarios for what can go wrong after a divorce are endless. If you've arrived in the LBC through divorce, you know exactly what we're talking about.

You've Had Some Health Problems

We hardly need to explain this scenario since it's been covered in the news so much. Your health insurer decides that the cancer that developed was a preexisting condition, never mind that you've been insured with them since 1985. They refuse to pay. Your treatments cost you $300,000 in medical bills, but you have no way to pay. Your credit score is soon destroyed.

You Bought a House with a Subprime Mortgage

We aren't judging you. Really. Even if you kept wondering at the closing what might happen when the housing payment went up too high in a few years, a lot of smart financial people—maybe your real estate agent and banker were among them—kept saying it was a good idea. It's understandable why you'd assume that if these really smart people who are trained in finances and real estate are saying that it's a good idea for you to buy this property, then it must be. Tens of millions of Americans learned this lesson the hard way during the subprime mortgage meltdown of 2008. Their credit scores will take years to recover.

You Took Out Too Many Credit Cards and Got in Over Your Head

If this describes you, you're hardly alone. It's been estimated that 215 million Americans have credit cards. No surprise there; but check this out: a 2007 study by the credit bureau Experian found that 14 percent of Americans had more than ten credit cards! (Our neighbors to the north, in case you're a Canadian reading this, have more than $50 billion on their credit cards.) So, what we're saying is that a lot of us have credit cards, and many of us have way too many of them.

You Didn't Do Anything Wrong; Your Credit Card Companies Turned on You

If you're one of these people, then you know exactly how this can happen. With a little notice, most credit card companies can change their rules and totally mess with your account. For instance, Jeanine Barone, a travel writer with stellar credit, has a Platinum American Express card and has had it for twenty years. She has never missed a payment, always sending in her money on time or early. "So you can imagine my surprise," says Barone, "when I tried to check out of a hotel in Madrid on a Monday morning to find that my card was declined."

She assumed it was an error but soon learned that, nope, no error. American Express had imposed a credit limit on her, one so low that she couldn't pay for the hotel. Once she learned that American Express had been given $3.39 billion by the U.S. Treasury in recent months, Barone was particularly steamed. But her situation isn't unique. In fact, the *New York Times* mentioned in a recent story that American Express began lowering credit limits for people who had *shopped* at places where other customers were routinely late in paying their bills.

JPMorgan Chase made a lot of customers angry when, for a time, they began adding a $10 monthly fee to low-interest cards that had carried large balances on them for the last two years. Fifth Third

Bank started handing customers who hadn't used their card in a year a $19 fee. But what has really hurt people's finances are the credit cards that have jacked up their interest rates, often by transferring customers from fixed rates to variable rates. If you think about it, ticking off your customers like that really is kind of an odd way to run a business. But as the saying goes, most bankers have never met a fee they didn't like.

You Lost Your Job

You can't very well pay your bills when you don't have money coming in. Downsizing, layoffs, corporate cost cutting . . . whatever they call it, it still stinks for the employees who are no longer getting a paycheck. Even for the few who had a comfortable rainy-day fund on hand, extended periods of unemployment will eventually sap all your resources. This happens to good employees all the time, and through no fault of their own, they suddenly find themselves with a stack of bills they cannot pay.

You Just Really Stink at Managing Your Money

Why is it that two people who earn the same salary can have vastly different financial situations? The reasons are complex and varied, but some financial experts say it boils down to this: one is a spender and one is a saver. Rare is the individual who will actually save for eighteen months to buy a new flat-screen television. But why save when the electronics store has no-interest financing for eighteen months, right? You can't listen to the radio without hearing one of those "no money down" commercials. America is a society of instant gratification; we want it now, even though we don't have the money to buy it now. So the truth is, savers are an endangered species, although they're making a comeback.

Let's face it, many of us are spenders, or have been. We like our four-dollar lattes, thirty-dollar haircuts, designer clothes, dining at nice restaurants, and going on vacation. It's the American way. And there's nothing wrong with that, if you have the money and you don't get carried away. Unfortunately, many people lose their way and have gotten in over their heads, enabled, of course, by the credit card companies, who keep urging us to get in over our heads.

However it happened and whatever your story is, you're not alone. According to a 2009 *Wall Street Journal* article, 110 million Americans now have bad credit. We're not math majors, but as far as we can tell, that's almost 50 percent of adults in this country. So by that ratio, for example, if you go to a party and there are twenty people there, odds are that ten of them have credit problems.

Also consider these statistics: In 2008, there were 3,157,806 foreclosures in the United States; in 2009, the foreclosure number went even higher. Also, in 2008 there were 1.67 million automobile repossessions and 1.1 million bankruptcies, with at least that many predicted for 2009.

Any way you look at it, the number of Americans with poor credit is soaring. It may not be a topic your friends write about on Facebook, but pick ten people you know, and we'll bet five of them have bad credit—even though they never talk about it.

In fact, as we've already said, one out of two of the authors of the book you're reading right now has bad credit—

Chris: Wait, hold on. This is going to get confusing, writing about ourselves in the third person.

Geoff: Don't worry, we'll figure it out. Maybe we'll do something eye-catching every once in a while, like break up some of the text with some formatted dialogue, like from a play.

Chris: I don't know—it sounds kind of hokey.

Geoff: Then we'll do it sparingly.

So, as we were saying, one of the two authors has bad credit right now and is trying to climb out of it with the rest of you. The other author, it may make you feel better to know, has a very high credit score (though it wasn't always that way). In any case, let's go with some brief introductions. Chris Balish is a former television news anchor—

Geoff: Wait, here's an idea. Why don't we really throw this book into disarray and go with first person?

Chris: Hey, it's our book. Why not? We'll introduce ourselves in first person, and then for the rest of the book, we'll go back to mostly doing this in third person.

Geoff: Okay, you want to go first? Besides, writing this book was your idea.

Chris: All right, then. Here goes . . .

CHRIS BALISH

First, thanks for reading our book. We appreciate it, because we know you'd rather be reading *Twilight* or watching *American Idol*. Thinking about your credit issues, while necessary, is probably not something you look forward to. That's why we're going to make this book as enjoyable a read as we can, as well as practical. And plenty of ideas for navigating the choppy water of bad credit are coming in the following pages.

As we mentioned earlier, my credit score is pretty healthy at the moment—at least it was the last time I checked. But as you well know, that can change in an instant. A couple of bad decisions, an ill-advised major purchase, corporate downsizing, a medical emergency, lapsed insurance, car crash, lost wallet . . . no one is immune to the life events that can wreak havoc on your FICO score.

I was inspired to cowrite this book for a couple of reasons. First, I remember several times in my life when a lack of credit embarrassed me so badly I literally broke into a cold sweat. I'll discuss some of those instances in the sidebars appearing throughout these pages. Back then my lack of credit caused me pain and shame, but now I have a totally different outlook.

Second, more than half of my friends have bad credit. Way more. And this has personally affected me in several ways; check out the sidebars for some funny stories about my kooky friends. Hint: I've had more than a few buddies couch surfing in my living room for months at a time because of bad credit issues. And my friends are not unusual. In fact, I didn't know so many of them had credit problems until I started researching this book; that's when the truth came out. You may not know it, but probably more than half of your friends also have bad credit; they just don't talk about it.

Third, as a professional journalist and hard-core news junkie, I closely followed the recession, which began in earnest in 2008, although in the technical sense, economists place it as beginning in December 2007. While lately my career has taken me into producing and hosting television shows, for ten years prior I was a television journalist, anchoring the local news in Cincinnati and St. Louis and being an on-air expert guest for cable networks like MSNBC and CNN. So I've covered a lot of financial topics over the years and interviewed hundreds of financial experts. And I've found myself riveted by what I've seen in the media, not to mention how my friends and family have been affected by the changing economy. So I found myself wanting to try to do something to help the millions of people who had their credit rating steamrolled by the recession of 2008–2009.

And finally, I've always been a student of personal finance and a longtime reader of magazines like *Kiplinger's* and *Money*. My first book was largely about personal finance; in fact, I believe most bookstores shelve it in the personal finance section. *How to Live Well Without Owning a Car* spends a big chunk of its time showing people how much money they can save by going car free or car-lite.

Not that I'm going to try in these pages to convince you to sell your car or not buy a new one—but it was an eye-opening experience for me to see how my finances were affected in such a positive way when I stopped spending so much money on transportation. So personal finance is an area of interest for me; I enjoy reading and writing about it, especially when I can help others by sharing what I've learned. And while my credit score is in good shape now, I've been in way over my head when it comes to debt, and I've often wondered what would have happened if I hadn't sold my SUV and started taking drastic steps to try get my finances under control.

One day it hit me that millions of people could benefit from a book like *How to Live Well with Bad Credit*. I spent a week going to bookstores in the Los Angeles area and learned that while there are plenty of books about how to improve your credit score, there was not one book about how to live well in the meantime. Do you have to put your life on hold, waiting for a better day? Heck no. We want you to live your best life *now*, even if your credit sucks at the moment. When I was discussing this idea with my literary agent, she said, "You're right! I love the idea, but I think you need a coauthor, someone with solid personal finance credentials. You know, you should meet Geoff Williams. He's a personal finance writer with a pretty interesting story."

Geoff and I talked on the phone, hit it off, and decided to work together on this project. And I couldn't be happier with the partnership. Geoff's expertise and skill-set perfectly complement mine, and he really knows this topic from his own reporting and firsthand experience. So here's Geoff on Geoff.

GEOFF WILLIAMS

I'm a personal finance writer who had to declare bankruptcy.

There, I said it.

This is the first time I've admitted this in print, so, yeah, I'll say it again right now—I had to declare bankruptcy. I assure you, my mom and dad are cringing and thinking, "Okay, we won't be telling anyone about this book." Most of my friends and family, if they're reading this, are learning about my bankruptcy for the first time. Some of my ex-girlfriends are thinking, "Whew, I dodged a bullet." Ah, this is fun.

I waved the white flag of surrender to my creditors about eighteen months before my agent introduced me to Chris Balish. Of course, anybody reading this has every right to wonder about the wisdom of reading a personal finance book where one of the authors has declared bankruptcy. But as we said earlier, this isn't a "how to become rich" book. We're not suggesting stock tips. We're not telling you how to invest your money. There's no magical formula in this book that we're going to ask you to follow. What we're doing—based on a lot of reporting and a lot of personal experience—is sharing what we know about living well with bad credit. And, believe me, this is a topic I know way too much about.

It also might be helpful for you to know that I wasn't a personal finance writer who, while telling readers how to spend their money, mismanaged his own and had to declare bankruptcy. I was a freelance magazine journalist who wrote about a variety of topics, from business articles for *Entrepreneur* to a parenting column in *BabyTalk*, and then began veering into writing about personal finance only after I was well on the road toward my own bankruptcy. I wanted to understand more about how credit cards work, how banks operated, and how credit card counseling firms dispersed money to creditors. So I started interviewing financial experts and researching topics that I found interesting, and soon I was writing for publications as diverse as AOL's personal finance blog, WalletPop, Bankrate.com, and CreditCards.com. And when I had a feature on credit cards appear in *Consumer Reports,* I felt like I had truly arrived as a personal finance writer.

I was interested in debt because it had consumed my life. The debt I had amassed before meeting my wife, who brought a little credit card debt of her own into our finances, was on my mind when I woke up and when I went to bed at night. I thought about it during work and away from work. Heck, don't tell my wife, but I probably thought about it when we—well, you know.

I worried about our finances even more when our daughters,

Isabelle and Lorelei, came along. I'd take them to the park on Saturdays, and while I watched them scamper on the playground, I'd sit there and also pay my bills in my head: *Okay, I can pay the $148 minimum monthly payment on my VISA, but I know I need to do more than that. If I pay $225, like I want to do, will I have enough to pay the $78 monthly payment on my MasterCard? And what about the $103.54 MBNA monthly payment—when am I going to give them that, and if I pay that this week, can I pay the electric bill? No, I can't pay the electric bill, but they won't turn it off until next month, so you can skip the electric this week. And don't forget, you still need to make your health insurance payment for the month . . .*

So, yes, debt has been a big part of my life, and I'm the first to admit that I've made some extremely foolish decisions over the years. One could easily argue that my biggest mistake—although I don't regret it—was deciding to become a freelance magazine writer. While the majority of the publications I've written for have paid me pretty quickly, I chose a profession where you can write an article for a magazine and be assured that you'll be paid in a month—then not get the check for another six months. It's also a career where you're beholden to the postal service. I'll never forget a neighbor once interrupting me while I was mowing our lawn, bringing me an envelope, saying, "The postman brought it to our house by mistake. It's been sitting in our kitchen for two weeks. I hope it isn't important."

It was a check for $500.

Once, the postal service took ten days to bring a $1,250 check that *Entrepreneur* magazine had sent to me. I was so rattled that for two years afterward, I paid *Entrepreneur* to Fed-Ex my checks to me.

My irregular cash flow and my wife's decision to stay home and watch our kids, which I did not discourage, along with growing credit card debt that needed to be paid off every month, regardless of whether I had a good month or not . . . well, it was a strategy that didn't work out well for me.

I first started to amass credit card debt when I was twenty-two, several months out of college, living on my own in Los Angeles, a kid from Ohio trying to make it big as a screenwriter; and from there, I'd say I made almost every financial mistake one can make. I was twenty-three when I lent $5,000 to my younger brother, who wound up trying to start a pie-selling business (yeah, really). That didn't go too well, and he wound up owing a baker $5,000. Now that I'm pushing forty, I look back at that memory of my twenty-three-year-old self and scream, "Noooooo! Don't do it!"

But I did. During a visit to see my family in my hometown, Middletown, Ohio, my brother suggested we take a walk in our neighborhood. Somewhere along the well-manicured lawns, he told me how he owed this bakery $5,000. It was quite a story, full of a lot of details that I no longer remember and don't care to try to recall. But he was afraid to tell our parents, and my mother must have cosigned the loan or something, because I remember him telling me how he was afraid her car was going to be repossessed if this $5,000 wasn't paid, and suddenly I was agreeing to front him $5,000 on my brand-new MBNA credit card stamped with a logo from my alma mater, Indiana University.

I think about that now in sheer disbelief. I agreed to loan the money to a twenty-one-year-old college kid with no job other than his failing business. I'm beyond sure now that if I had gone to my parents, we would have avoided a lot of problems.

But I also look back at my twenty-three-year-old self and wonder why, a few months before lending my brother money, I bought a $20,000 Ford Probe that I couldn't possibly afford, which will forevermore be referred to as the Second Dumbest Financial Decision Ever Made. I was working full-time at a magazine, but I was making just a little more than $20,000 at the time, and here I was, buying a car worth a year's salary.

No problem, I thought at the time. *The payments are kind of steep, but I'll take on some extra work and write freelance articles and pay for the car that way.*

I'm getting a migraine just thinking of my logic back then.

Not that I didn't make some stupid decisions in my thirties. I made a couple of momentous ones, but by that time, I knew they were dumb. But money can be very emotional, leading to a lot of desperate feelings when you don't have enough of it, and sometimes, even when you know you shouldn't, you give in to the idiocy.

I remember one year, it was December 23, and we had almost no money in our bank account to buy gifts. Our daughter, Isabelle, had been born a couple of months before, and even though logically I knew that she wouldn't notice or care if there weren't gifts under the tree—nor would my wife, parents, or brother—it was eating away at me. And then that day, a check from Wells Fargo came in the mail. I don't remember the exact amount, but the check was for something like $1,023.

I hadn't written anything for Wells Fargo. No, apparently, they were sending these to anyone with a pulse. If I cashed it, the letter attached to the check told me, I could have the money instantly and would just have to pay $42 a month for the next three years. (I can't swear that it was $42 a month, but whatever it was, it would add up to well over $1,023 by the time I finished paying them.)

I had received these checks numerous times and ripped them up. But on December 23, 2001, I was weak. Trembling, cursing myself, I drove up to my ATM in the evening, made a deposit, adding $1,023 to what was probably $40 in our checking account, and then drove to the mall. I promised myself during that trip that I would finally go see a credit counseling service, which I did, several days later. I enrolled in the nonprofit's debt-paying service, where I paid the service, and they dispersed my money to my creditors. But because I didn't carefully vet the credit counseling service, that decision, too, had its consequences.

Several years later, I argued with my wife about declaring bankruptcy. She understandably refused. It's not a decision one makes lightly. I also brought up the idea to my father, who thought I was crazy. Respecting both their opinions, I shelved the idea, but a couple of years after those conversations, when we took out another loan with a lending company, desperate for cash to keep up with our credit cards, I had a sinking feeling that we were putting off the inevitable.

By the time I finally declared bankruptcy at the age of thirty-eight, sixteen years after giving that loan to my brother, which we still hadn't fully paid off, I had tried just about everything that personal finance writers beg you not to.

BUT IT'S NOT SO BAD IN THE LAND OF BAD CREDIT

We debated about putting the above as a subhead to this book. There are a lot of horror stories out there, and we don't want to minimize or make light of that by implying that bad credit is no big deal. But in some ways, it really isn't so bad. Let's check in at the end of the book and see if you agree with us.

If You Already Have Bad Credit, You No Longer Have to Live in Fear of Losing Your Good Credit Score

The journey to bad credit can be a lot more stressful and anxiety-causing than reaching the actual destination. The bark is worse than the bite, as they say. We're *not* saying you shouldn't care about your credit score, or if you make a late payment. Late payments usually mean fees, and you have better things to spend your money on than fees.

But, look, when you had great credit and were paying bills late, you had a lot to lose and probably felt sick about everything. Now it's like you're driving a 1985 Buick that still runs fine but has a few dents. A few more dings may make the car look a little worse, but there's no use stressing about it.

Stop for a Moment and Think About How Lucky You Are

Yes, that may sound like lunacy, especially if you've lost your house, your car, and just about everything, but we're talking big picture here. You're reading this book, trying to improve things. We all have something that we value, whether it's our health or our sense of humor. You may have lost a lot, but hopefully you still have what means the most to you—the important things in life, like your friends, family, and that box of *MAD* magazines stashed in the basement. Or maybe you and your family are living with your parents at the moment, and while that's not ideal, your mother and father probably now mean even more to you, since they're helping you in your time of need.

Chris: And remember what Oprah says, "Just to live in this country, you are ahead of 95 percent of the world's people."

Geoff: What a fine, smart, intelligent woman.

Chris: You're sucking up, hoping she mentions our book on her show, aren't you?

Geoff: Of course not (*aside*, *stage whisper:* Oprah, call me).

It's when things are the worst that we need to take stock of what we do have. If you're struggling to manage your money, it may be even more important to manage your stress. Seriously, don't forget that.

If you're feeling stressed about all of the bills that you have to pay but don't have the money to pay, you're entitled to some well-earned anxiety. But you're also entitled to take a break, relax, and take a look around every so often and feel good about what's going well in your life.

You Have Nowhere to Go but Up

Yes, it's technically true that things could get worse—you could always get hit by a truck (literally or figuratively). Maybe you're reading this book while waiting to learn the fate of your house or car. But let's be positive, people! Hopefully you're reading this at a point when the worst is over, and you're just trying to figure out what to do now. If that's the case, savor this moment. Enjoy it. Seriously, look around, take stock of your surroundings, eat a cupcake, and relax—things are about to improve. If you're at rock bottom now, better times lay ahead. That should give you some sense of relief. In fact, for some people, bad credit can be the start of a new beginning.

For Alexis Moore, of El Dorado Hills, California, overall it's been a positive experience. Moore declared bankruptcy in March 2006 after a nasty breakup, in which her significant other took her credit cards and added $70,000 to her $30,000 debt. Moore, then thirty-two, tried to resolve the debts that she hadn't accrued, but ultimately when one creditor decided to sue her, and having no luck getting the law authorities to help her (she filed numerous reports with the FTC, FBI, the police, and the district attorney's office), she decided it was time to declare bankruptcy.

And, indeed, bankruptcy, for Moore, was the fresh start that it was intended to be for people. She ended up leaving her career of real estate, enrolling in law school, and forming a nonprofit group for victims of domestic violence called Survivors in Action. She describes her life after 2006 as "the best time of my life."

Since not just the $70,000 was erased from her obligations, but her own debt as well, Moore has found that she no longer stresses out over money and bills. "I did what I could afford at first, because I was forced to, but now it's a way of life," says Moore, who is perfectly happy with her VISA debit card. "I have learned that there's a lot a person can do without credit."

However you got here, you're here, and it's not so bad, is it? You may have a score of 513 or 499, but the world hasn't come to an end. Your family and friends still love you. You're hopefully still getting three square meals a day. And, unlike in some far-flung countries where one bad check can land you in debtor's prison, you haven't been shackled and tossed into a cell.

Chris: Does that still happen in the world?

Geoff: Yes. Google it. And stop looking over my shoulder.

We heard from a fifty-three-year-old man in Florida named William. His credit problems were so bad he was being sued by a half dozen creditors and eventually had his wages garnished, and he is currently living on 75 percent of his state government salary. In the midst of this, he got a divorce from his wife. After a turbulent adjustment period, to put it mildly, even William is optimistic.

"Try to think of it as temporary," he says of having bad credit. "It is, if you want it to be. And use this time as an opportunity to improve yourself and to learn new things, such as gardening, cooking, canning, and how to be a better shopper. Clip coupons. Get into walking instead of going to the movies. Focus on free stuff. Become very practical, something Americans have mostly lost. Being a history fan, I imagine how much my grandparents and parents lived through during the depression and World War II, doing without, but seemingly coming through it better for having had the experience, and not necessarily being bitter and broken."

And now that you are in bad credit territory, have you noticed that a lot of organizations and companies are clamoring for your attention? When you were on your long slide down into the Land of Bad Credit, you were kind of invisible—but no more. There are a lot of reputable organizations that really, truly want to do business with you and help you rebuild your credit. On the other hand, of course, there are also plenty of dishonest enterprises and scam artists that will tell you they want to help your credit, but really, as soon as you look the other way, they just want to help themselves to what money you still have.

Yes, it's great to be wanted.

Fun Fact to Bore Your Friends
with at Parties

Today, your FICO score ranges from 300 to 850—300 being the worst and 850 being the ultimate best. But it used to be that your credit score went from 1 to 9. If you had a 1, you had an incredible credit history, whereas 8 and 9 meant your credit standing was in tatters.

BANKING WITH BAD CREDIT

Yes. Money has been a little tight lately.
But, at the end of my life, when I'm sitting on
my yacht, am I gonna be thinking about how much
money I have? No. I'm going to be thinking about
how many friends I have, and my children,
and my comedy albums. I mean, I have a yacht,
so I obviously did pretty well moneywise.

MICHAEL SCOTT (PLAYED BY STEVE CARELL), DISCUSSING HIS
FINANCIAL TROUBLES IN NBC'S SITCOM, *THE OFFICE*

LIKE MANY OF YOU, we have mixed feelings about banks. There
have been times when we've wondered if pickpockets were now
managing the store, given how deep the bank overdraft fees have
dug into our checking accounts. Meanwhile, ATMs charge you to
access your own money, and a few banks have even devised fees for
talking to a teller or customer service representative on the phone.

On the other hand, the tellers give candy to our kids and treats to our dogs when we go through the drive-through. Sometimes you'll get a toaster, or these days, an iPod, for opening up an account. They pay us interest—a little, anyway—if we put our money in a savings account. And it's hard to undo the image of the staid, but dependable banker George Banks in *Mary Poppins,* singing about how "soon that tuppence, safely invested in the bank, will compound." Or if you're of a certain age, you might fondly remember Mr. Theodore J. Mooney from Lucille Ball's 1960s series, *The Lucy Show.* He was this often-irritated, pompous banker, but you never got the feeling he was anything but full of integrity.

So whether you love 'em or hate 'em, banks are an integral part of the financial system, and they're here to stay, and while we know some people will disagree, we're of the mind-set that you're better off with them than without them. So if you don't have a bank account or are thinking of abandoning yours, well, hopefully you'll hear us out.

CHEXSYSTEMS

If you've been turned down for a bank account repeatedly, then you're almost surely in the database known as ChexSystems. This company is to banks what a bouncer is to a nightclub. ChexSystems tells banks whether you should be allowed in or not, by placing people who have had trouble with banks in their database. This can be a great thing, of course. There are plenty of con artists out there who purposely write bad checks, and that's why the company came into existence. And we should be grateful for ChexSystems: clods who try to game the system raise the cost of banking for the rest of us.

ChexSystems began in Minneapolis, Minnesota, in 1971. The intention was to keep criminals from writing bad check after bad check and then opening up a new bank account elsewhere. It was a needed service, and while they mostly serviced banks in Minnesota and Wisconsin in the early and mid-1970s, one can see why and how they spread across the nation.

The problem, critics say, and we agree, is that sometimes the punishment is far worse than the crime. Many people who get into this company's national database aren't criminals hoping to steal thousands or millions—they're people who mismanaged their money. Mismanagement, of course, might not even be a fair term, given how banks like to structure their payment system.

We probably don't need to tell you this, but banks have figured out very nicely how to capitalize on their customers' mistakes. If you wind up using your debit card too often, well, here's what can happen: Let's say that you've been using your debit card pretty freely because you have $100 in the bank, but your spouse has a tire blowout on the road and calls in a tow truck. We'll assume you might have road service—but your panicked spouse thinks there's more in the account and spends $250 to replace a couple of tires.

If the banks put the customer first, they would either decline your card, and you'd pay for your tires another way, or they'd run the smallest debts through first and go with the biggest last. They don't, though. They take the biggest debts out of your checking account first.

So let's say that you went shopping on a given day, spending $7 at Panera Bread, $22.18 at the grocery store, $30 at the gas station, 99 cents for a ringtone, and you made a $10 payment to www.meal pay.com (a website that a lot of schools use for parents to pay their kids' school lunches). Now, if the bank ran those five charges through first, you'd still have almost $80 left. Then the $250 tires would go through. You'd have one hefty overdraft charge.

But, of course, most of the banks don't do that. They run the $250 charge through first, putting you $150 in the negative. There's your first overdraft charge. Then those other five charges go through, so that you have six more overdraft charges. At about $35 a pop, that's a pretty sickening $210 in bank fees. And if you don't have a paycheck coming, you're now going to remain $310 in the negative. And God forbid that the $10 check you gave your child for a school fundraiser goes through tonight. If it does, there's another $35 fee.

Now, look, you probably shouldn't have been going to Panera Bread and buying ringtones with so little in the bank, and your spouse definitely should have been paying more attention to the checking account. The banks are right to expect you to keep track of your money—and it's understandable that they would want to charge customers who can't keep track of things. But how they meter out penalties and fees has been just plain greedy—and it's why government oversight is needed to protect customers—and why banks, as of late, have been changing their ways.

If You're in the ChexSystems Database

You may have concluded that you can't open a bank account because you've been turned down by several banks, but you're probably looking in the wrong places. If you aren't sure if you're in the ChexSystems database, or just want to see what information they have about you, you're entitled to a free report from them once a year, which you can get by going to www.consumerdebit.com.

ChexSystems services 80 percent of the banks in the country. That's a lot, but there are still 20 percent of the FDIC-insured banks and credit unions remaining that don't use ChexSystems. If you want a checking account, you need to hunt around and find one of those.

Or you can go to ChexSystems' home page (https://www.consumer debit.com), or whatever bank you want to apply to, and ask to be admitted into their Second Chance program. You'll have to participate in their mandatory money management course, and you'll be given a new, restricted checking account. You have to pay a fee— usually around $10 a month—for about six months, which is the probation period. If you avoid bounced checks and overdrafts during those six months, then you no longer have to pay the $10 fee, and you aren't on probation (so if you wind up with more overdraft fees, you won't be kicked out).

Now, we understand that you may be kind of irked—after all, the banks gave you fees that helped you get into your mess, and now they want more fees? If that's how you feel, as we said, there are banks that don't use ChexSystems that would be happy to have you as a customer—or it may just be time to suck it up and go through the program. But whatever you do, you should have a bank account. Here's why.

THE UNBANKED

In early 2008, former president Bill Clinton and California governor Arnold Schwarzenegger had an eye-opening column in the *Wall Street Journal,* called "Beyond Payday Loans" (January 24, 2008 issue). They wrote at length about people who don't have a bank account—more than 20 million Americans. Some estimates put the number closer to 30 million. These folks are referred to in the banking industry as "the unbanked."

The very word kind of conjures up images of subhuman zombies—the undead, the unbanked—or maybe we've just been watching too many horror movies lately. If you're a member of the unbanked—and there are an increasing number of professionals out there who are—the column in the *Wall Street Journal* had some jaw-dropping statistics: more than $8 billion a year is "spent at check-cashing outlets, payday lenders and pawnshops on basic financial services that most Americans receive for free—or very little cost—at their local bank or credit union. Over a lifetime, the average full-time, unbanked worker will spend more than $40,000 just to turn his or her salary into cash."

Of course, an unbanked person might just as easily retort that in 2009, more than $38.5 billion in overdraft fees were collected by banks. You do the math. Still, the argument for sticking it out with a bank is that if you can get your finances under control, you won't pay overdraft charges. If you don't get a bank account, you'll always be stuck paying those fees.

THE MIDDLE GROUND

There are some other considerations. If you want a checking account but are fearful of making an error that will cost you a lot of cash in bank fees, Probity Financial Services might be worth checking out. They're a financial services firm that offers online banking, and they partner with several FDIC-insured banks. Their big selling point is that they have no overdraft fees. None. If you go into the negative, they'll put all your charges through to $500, and you just get your money back into the positive when you can. How can they do that? Well, they have a monthly account maintenance fee of $19.95.

This isn't exactly a bargain—you're paying $239.40 a year to have a checking account. Over a decade, that's $2,394. But do the math: if you're paying more than $239 a year in checking-cash fees or overdraft fees, it might be your most affordable option. It won't work very well, however, for self-employed people, like the authors of this book, because if you want your money quickly, you have to have direct deposit to use Probity. If you work for a company that does direct deposit, then everything is like a regular bank, only without the brick-and-mortar building to go into. You'll get a MasterCard debit card, and you'll just do all of your banking online. You can make additional deposits at ATMs or through the mail. On the downside, you will get hit by an ATM fee, which is why Probity's website advises its customers to "ask for 'cash back' when making purchases with your debit card." If you do that, you'll get no fees, and you can still have cash on hand.

There are some online banking websites like TheMoneyBox.com, that offer a full range of banking and checking account services, but in return they take 1 percent of everything you deposit. That doesn't sound like much at first, but if you make, say, $50,000 a year in salary, after taxes you're giving them about $400 annually, or $33 a month. That's still less than some people spend in overdraft fees, which is why we're mentioning them. So it may make sense under the right circumstances. But 1 percent of your hard-earned income to go to your bank? Every year? The best thing you can do for your finances is to find a traditional FDIC-insured bank or credit union and then do everything you can to stay in their good graces.

STAYING IN A BANK'S GOOD GRACES

If you're going to use a bank account and want to protect yourself from bank fees, here are some strategies.

Use Cash

If you're afraid you can't trust yourself with the debit card, and that something is going to go wrong, this is a tried and true plan that works. The country used to get along without debit cards just fine. Many people do this, not because they have to, but as a matter of choice; lots of Chris's friends are cash-only, incidentally, and never use plastic.

That said, using debit cards is ingrained in our national psyche now, and it isn't an easy habit to break. So if you occasionally lack self-discipline—like, um, the authors of this book—try this: wrap your debit card in aluminum foil before sticking it in your purse or wallet. Or place it in a sealed envelope. Then you'll have your debit card if there's an emergency, but you'll be reminded not to use it. (Just remember that a pair of Manolo Blahnik shoes on sale is not an emergency.) The foil should serve as an effective reminder of what you're trying to avoid if you reach for your plastic to buy those shoes, or even a Slurpy that you haven't budgeted for.

And that's why it's a great idea to use cash—to help us budget. A lot of people started using their debit cards more than credit cards when the Great Recession kicked in. More people in 2009, in fact, were using debit cards than credit cards, which was the first time that ever happened. Well, it's no wonder a record amount of over-draft fees were collected. We've been using debit cards like credit cards—stick it in the gas pump and decide to get $16 worth of gas—

well, no, let's make it an even $20—naw, how about $25? Debit cards just make it too easy to spend money.

You can't pump gas like that if you're only carrying cash. If you have $20 on you, you're hopefully not going to let yourself pump more than $20 in gas, and chances are, you'll stick to your original $16 plan, knowing you want to keep a few bucks in your wallet just in case. If we buy just about everything with debit cards, and spend a few bucks more on many or most of our purchases, well, no wonder so many of us often come up short at the end of the month.

Get to Know Your Bank Tellers

This isn't foolproof by any means, and if you've had problems with overdraft fees, you may be well ahead of us on this. Bank tellers and managers are much more likely to give you a break on fees if they know who you are. If you make it clear that you're really trying to manage your bank account, they're even more likely to refund some of your money. It won't always work if it happens frequently, but if there's a problem and you're in a gray area—like that ninety-nine-cent ringtone charge, c'mon—a bank manager is probably going to side with you, if they know you and you don't treat them like a jerk.

One of Geoff's wife's relatives even occasionally takes a home-made plate of cookies for his bank tellers, knowing that it might foster goodwill that he may need later. That seems a little unnecessary to one's dignity—after all, they probably know exactly what he's doing—but there's definitely something to treating your bank teller and manager like a human being.

Learn How Your Bank Works

Banks are complicated institutions. Their policies change frequently to keep up with an evolving marketplace and an ever-changing economy. Even bank managers have trouble keeping up. We know you're not going to read the bank's policy manual, and it's easy to not pay attention to the statements and literature they send. But you should have a fundamental understanding of how your bank works.

Even if you do ignore the written material, and we can hardly blame you, if you don't understand how something works—like why you pump $15 of gas, but it only shows up as $1 on your bank's website—ask your teller what's going on. The bank is holding and handling *your* money. You have every right to understand how they process fees. More important, if you understand how they process fees, that may help you avoid an error later.

Use Automatic Withdrawals Sparingly

This gets tougher as time goes by because so many companies love pitching automatic withdrawal as a convenient way to pay your bill. And we all have so many monthly bills these days. Your wireless carrier likes automatic withdrawal. Your mortgage company, of course, prefers it. Your car and health insurance, and just about every company with which you do business would like to sign you up for their automatic withdrawal program.

Some bills probably are best left to automatic withdrawal. If your health and car insurance are automatically withdrawn, you're always covered, and you haven't left to chance the possibility that you might forget or not be able to pay later and lose the insurance coverage.

But, gee, if you forget to pay your newspaper or cable bill and you lose it, what's the worst that happens? You pay for it after your lose it, and then you get it back. Keep in mind that when you have a lot of automatic withdrawals, the places you pay your bills to are dictating how and when you're spending your money, instead of you making that choice. Granted, you may have the type of organized mind that loves automatic withdrawal, and if it works for you, great—keep at it.

But if you're not so organized, remember that unless you're really careful with your money, automatic withdrawals—especially if they're sporadic and easily forgotten—can be a common cause of overdrafts. At the very least, they could put you in a situation where you suddenly have less money in the bank than you planned. Chris has found a convenient way to keep track of all of his automatic withdrawals. He simply creates a repeating calendar entry on his computer so that every month he can see which bills are being withdrawn when. The amounts vary slightly, but in general he knows his cable bill is paid on the twentieth, and that it will be around $150, give or take.

Geoff: Your cable bill is $150. Why so high?

Chris: Are you always this nosy?

Use Those Automatic Transfer Savings Plans Sparingly, Too

A lot of banks—to their credit—promote savings. Some of these plans are pretty creative, too. With every debit card purchase, one dollar is automatically ferreted off to your savings account. Or with every debit card or credit card purchase, the price is rounded up to the next dollar and funneled off to your savings account. In many ways, that's great—obviously, we all need to save money, and if you have bad credit, you may need to save now more than ever. But keep in mind that if you're constantly getting into overdraft protection, you've set it up so that you're going to have even less money from day-to-day in your checking account, increasing the odds that one of these days, you're going to go into overdraft. By all means, sock money into a savings account—it's just that you may want to do it within your own time frame and in the amount you know you can handle, rather than letting the bank decide for you.

Ask for Overdraft Protection

This is a great feature that you should do everything in your power to get attached to your checking account. It really could save you a lot of money. For example, Chris has $500 in overdraft protection on his checking account—essentially it's a $500 line of credit that only kicks in if he goes below a zero balance. So if Chris writes a check for $800 but there's only $700 in his checking account, the extra $100 is pulled from the line of credit. No $35 overdraft fees. This feature saves his butt at least two or three times a year.

But overdraft protection is a form a credit, and if your credit history is not so great at the moment, you might have to work a little to convince your bank to give it to you. You may have to ask repeatedly. You may want to call someone higher than the bank manager, if you're told no.

Geoff had many problems with bank fees over the years, first with Provident Bank, which was then bought by National City, and later was swallowed up by PNC. Within several months of his first visit to a bankruptcy attorney, right about the time everything else financial in his life was imploding, Geoff's overdraft problem became so great that he wound up leaving National City and opening up a new account at another big, shiny bank down the street, fully intending to pay back National City. It never quite worked out that way. He is still in the ChexSystems database and expects to be for some time, but he is still with the big, shiny bank down the street—and, well, even after joining the hall of shame with ChexSystems, he was nevertheless accepted into a local credit union.

But the point of the story is this: Geoff didn't try hard enough to get overdraft protection on his account, although he did try several times over the course of almost a decade. If he could have succeeded sooner, it would have saved him a lot of money and a lot of hassle. The big, shiny bank down the street finally gave him overdraft protection after a long, heartfelt conversation with the bank manager the day after Geoff got smacked with about eight overdraft fees. Finally, after about fifteen minutes of conversation, the manager suggested that they link Geoff's checking account with a savings account. She said if he put some of his own money aside into the savings account, and some expenses triggered an overdraft, they would take money out of the savings account. There would still be an overdraft fee, but at only $10 a pop. Sounded like a nice compromise. The bank didn't have to extend credit, but Geoff would still be protected.

Geoff stared at the bank manager for a moment. He blinked. Geoff had requested overdraft protection numerous times, but never had been offered anything like this. Minutes later, he heard the bank manager whisper to the assistant manager, "We're not supposed to offer this unless the customer specifically asks for it."

Geoff just shook his head, slightly bewildered at having found the secret to getting overdraft protection. Apparently, it helps when your voice cracks, and the bank manager thinks she is about to witness a grown, middle-aged man about to cry. But you don't have to pretend to cry. Just ask, very directly, if you can have overdraft protection, in which you fund your line of credit yourself. And happily, it's getting easier, and not harder, to get that overdraft protection because of all the backlash banks have had in recent years.

The Pros and Cons of Prepaid Cards

The appeal of prepaid cards is easy enough to understand—they look and behave like credit cards, but you don't need a bank account to use one. They're aimed at people who are afraid to go into debt with a credit card, and at the unbanked, who no longer have access to a debit card. If you don't want to carry cash around, prepaid cards may seem like a pretty nice alternative. But keep in mind that there are fees attached.

They work like this. You load your own money onto a prepaid card, which you can then use to swipe at the supermarket for groceries or to buy stuff online. But then you get hit with some fees. Put another way, you're paying Walmart, Visa, and these other companies a small sum of cash every month to hang on to *your* money, which they're going to collect a little interest on. It's another cost of not having a proper checking account, but many people who have no other options are happy to pay the fees.

But these fees add up. You may have an activation fee, a monthly fee, a yearly fee, an ATM withdrawal fee, and even a fee every time you swipe it to make a purchase. Some annual fees can be as high as $99, and monthly fees can be as much as $10. And with some prepaid cards, you can even find yourself in overdraft territory. If purchases aren't posted right away, and you spend more than your card balance, you could get hit with a *shortage fee* that might be as high as $29.

But prepaid cards have their proponents, so if you swear by them, you probably already know that Walmart's prepaid card is one of the best options out there. Their low-cost prepaid card has a $3 activation fee, a $3 monthly fee, and a $2 ATM withdrawal fee. Visa also has several "UPSide" prepaid cards for teens and parents that have pretty good rates.

Still, again, you're paying these companies money to keep your money. You want to hang on to your money for as long as you can, but you lose some of it the moment you put it onto a prepaid card. Consumers Union, which publishes *Consumer Reports,* recently put out a devastating report on prepaid cards entitled "Prepaid Cards: Second-Tier Bank Account Substitutes" (you can read the full article at http://www.consumer-action.org/radar/articles/prepaid _cards_new_report/).

Here's the beginning of their report: "Prepaid cards, or 'general purpose reloadable cards,' are marketed as sensible, attractive alternatives to cashier's checks and traditional bank accounts. However, consumers face dangers and traps with prepaid cards, which are becoming the foundation of a second-tier banking system that shadows the traditional banking system. Until consumers who use prepaid cards are guaranteed the same protections as consumers who use traditional debit and credit cards, consumers who use prepaid cards will be at the risk of losing all their money, face multiple, high, and sometimes confusing fees, and be offered convenient but very expensive forms of credit associated with the card."

Despite all that, there are some arguments in favor of getting a prepaid card. If you don't have a bank of your own and refuse to get one, and thus don't have a debit or credit card, a prepaid card can work out well when accessing a plane ticket, rental car, or hotel. These businesses often demand some kind of plastic. But be aware that not all hotels and rental car companies accept prepaid cards, which may be the very reason you got one in the first place. Call ahead to find out for sure.

There is one more benefit that prepaid cards have that you may prefer over cash. If someone steals your wallet, your cash is gone. But if your prepaid card is lost or stolen, you're usually only liable for the first $50. And if you call and report the problem within two business days, you'll probably get all of your money back, save that $50.

So all in all, we believe you're better off keeping your cash in a bank, where your money can sit safely and collect interest. If you're afraid of overdrafts and nonsufficient funds penalties, strictly use the cash method and maybe occasionally, if you must, like if you're traveling, put some of the money on a prepaid card.

The Payday Loan Paradox

BY GEOFF WILLIAMS

There has been a lot of negative press about payday loans, and one has to wonder if any of the journalists that decry these centers have ever had to use one. I have, and I can tell you that the media is right to tear the payday lending establishments apart—and completely wrong.

If you've been reading this book all the way through, or, heck, even if you've been skipping around, it probably won't come as a surprise to learn that I have used payday lending on occasion, and that Chris, my coauthor, has not. The first time I ever went into one of these stores—that's what they call them, payday lending "stores," which is pretty accurate because in a sense you're buying money—I felt completely humiliated. They don't have the best reputation in the world, and it felt like the bottom of the barrel. It probably didn't help that the place I visited, like most of them, I suspect, has a bulletproof partition between the customers and the staff. It's like an unspoken sign that reads, "You stay on your side where you belong."

According to the Center for Responsible Lending (www.responsiblelending.org), 12 million Americans are "caught in a cycle of 400% interest payday lending debt every year." Now, that doesn't really mean that for every $100 someone borrows, you pay $400. It's more like $15 per one hundred, at least at the place I've been to; there are places that will charge far higher. The numbers the Center for Responsible Lending use reflect what the cost of the loan will be if you don't pay the loan back within a year's time, or if you're constantly paying off the loan only to borrow the same amount again. That's why the media is right to trash payday lending centers: it's an easy way to get yourself into a revolving debt spiral.

Let's say that you take out $700 and you owe them $805. If a $2,000 paycheck comes, and you pay them $805, and you're left with $1,195 for the next week or so, you may do fine—or, if your mortgage is $1,200 and it's due, you may find yourself in a jam. So you take out another payday loan . . . and, well, you can see how this goes. And that's exactly what happened to me. After taking out my first payday loan, I was back twice within a month until I could finally rip myself free of the cycle. Several weeks later, however, I would go again, taking out a little less, and I found myself going back one more time within the month.

And what's really scary, according to the Center for Responsible Lending, the payday lending industry collects 90 percent of their revenue from borrowers who repeatedly renew or reopen their payday loans. They're counting on you staying indebted and addicted to them.

That's not to say I think payday lending is evil. If used sparingly, they can help out in a pinch. But I would treat it like you would a fire extinguisher: only use in an emergency. Otherwise, there's an awfully good chance you'll create an emergency—in which you're constantly trying to pay down your payday loan debt.

However you use credit, whether as a short-term stopgap or a student loan, it's useful to remember the wisdom from Dan Danford, CEO of the Family Investment Center in St. Joseph, Missouri, who is quoted elsewhere in this book: "Credit, by itself, isn't a bad thing. What makes it bad—or potentially bad—is that it snowballs. It grows all by itself. You give it life, and then it starts working against you."

GETTING A GOOD JOB WITH BAD CREDIT

How do you get out from under it?
You can't reestablish your credit if you
can't get a job, and you can't get a
job if you've got bad credit.

MATTHEW A. FINKIN, A SYMPATHETIC LAW PROFESSOR,
IN AN INTERVIEW IN THE *NEW YORK TIMES*, AUGUST 7, 2009

RALPH HIRSCH WAS A successful television news director until one day he wasn't. New management came into the Huntsville, Alabama, television station where Hirsch worked for almost three years and decided to bring in a new news director.

"That was his prerogative to lay me off, but I wish he hadn't done that," says Hirsch, speaking in a light Southern drawl. Hirsch was unceremoniously pushed into the job market during an economy that was rapidly deflating.

He filed for unemployment and quickly began sending out résumés—not just in the field of journalism but public relations and government as well. Occasionally, he would land a job interview, and in one case, he flew to Baltimore to discuss running a TV news operation. Everything went well, and the job seemed to be in the bag, until he flew back to Alabama. When he landed, he received a phone call and was told that while he was in flight, the company had frozen the position.

This economy, Hirsch later thought, *is eating people alive . . .*

In between sending out résumés—four hundred of them by Month Ten—Hirsch was taking photos and selling them to a website, getting about $400 a month from that. His unemployment check was keeping the family somewhat afloat. He had managed to land a temporary position as a news director at a TV station in Fort Meyers, Florida, for about four weeks. But none of it was enough. Month after month went by, with most of the bills paid, except for the mortgage.

But fortunately in Month Ten, Hirsch, who had unearthed every contact he had, spoke to a guy he had worked with twenty years earlier in Columbus, Ohio.

"I may know someone in Cincinnati who's looking for a news director," his colleague from twenty years back told him. "Maybe we can set something up."

Hirsch paled when he learned the proposed salary—a 50 percent pay cut. But he reasoned that half of what he used to make was better than nothing. Not like Hirsch had much of a choice. His 401(k) was gone, along with the rest of his family's savings.

"Silly me," says Hirsch. "I invested in a home."

Less than a week before he lost his home, Hirsch was offered a job as a television news director in Cincinnati. During the job application process, Hirsch had to ask the question everyone has to ask themselves when they have bad credit and are looking for a good job: *Do I tell my future employer about my situation or do I keep my mouth shut?*

Hirsch told them—and still got the job. He still isn't sure if it was beneficial to say anything or not. "If they checked my credit history, it was not a problem that they raised during the interview process," says Hirsch, "but I didn't hide anything. I think that's pretty important."

A HEADHUNTER'S VIEWPOINT

Waffles Natusch agrees with Hirsch's mind-set. As president of the Barrett Group, a global career management firm headquartered in Warwick, Rhode Island, when it comes to the topic of bad credit and careers, Natusch is at ground zero. Natusch's company helps executives find jobs, specializing particularly in helping executives change careers. In fact, while he has helped dozens and dozens of upstanding citizens find solid employment, Natusch has helped a lot of lost causes, from embezzling and convicted CEOs to disbarred attorneys, defrocked priests, and unlicensed doctors.

He knows a lot about what's in the dreaded background check and exactly what a hiring manager is going to see when it comes to your credit history. So you'll hear a lot from him in this chapter. And Natusch is a man who knows something about starting over with bad credit. It came up in the course of our interview that early in his career, due to his own poor money management, Natusch filed for bankruptcy. But he went on to marry a lovely schoolteacher and founded a multimillion-dollar firm. He's one of millions of examples of how people can fail big—and later succeed big.

The link between credit scores and job seeking these days, he concedes, is very real and in some ways paints a gloomy picture. "The average credit rating is going down, not up, and we have so many responsible professionals on the ropes, and often not of their own fault," says Natusch. "Hiring managers know that, of course, but so few jobs are being posted and filled, and there are so many applicants, many hiring managers see the bad credit angle as a good reason for weeding out a potential job applicant."

But don't get discouraged. Because even in the age of the Internet, most employers do *not* run credit checks on prospective employees. About 35 percent of the companies surveyed by the Society for Human Resource Management pulled credit reports of potential employees in 2008. That's up from 19 percent in 1996. But it also means that almost two-thirds of employers do not run credit checks. Also keep in mind that most government and high-security jobs, like FBI agent or armored truck driver, always run credit checks. There are plenty of professions remaining where there aren't credit checks. You can probably become a farm laborer, lifeguard, or a stripper without a credit check, or you could sell watches on Times Square, or . . . well, have you ever considered becoming a mime?

Chris: A *mime*? Did we really just write that?

Geoff: Oh, I'm crazy for suggesting people become a mime, but you're the man with the plan for telling people they should become a stripper or sell watches on Times Square . . .

Chris: You are right. You are so cool. I wish I was you.

Geoff: But, of course.

Chris: Stop rewriting what I wrote! Folks, I didn't write that Geoff was cool.

Geoff: What you wrote was unprintable! *(There is a struggle.)*

Ahem, so, yes, many professions—even some low-paying retail jobs—will put it out there that they may do a background check on you, which may or may not include looking at your credit history. But have peace of mind in the fact that the vast majority of employers do not pull your credit report. When you're interviewing for that big job, concentrate on doing your best; don't waste your time worrying about something that in all likelihood will never come into play. And remember, these days the highest percentage of people who won't pass a background check probably have the job title of CEO. Still, stories like Ralph Hirsch's should give you plenty of hope, and Natusch offers reasons to be optimistic. He lists three socially acceptable reasons for having bad credit:

1. **Medical emergencies.** "If you had a serious illness, and you were in the hospital for six months, and consequently driven into bankruptcy, you're likely to get a lot of sympathy."

2. **Divorce.** "Considering that more than half of us are getting divorces, nobody's likely to think less of you if a messy breakup wrecked your credit."

3. **Your financial ruin is due to a major news story.** "If you were a victim of a Ponzi scheme or other fraud, the way that some people were when Bernie Madoff's scheme came to light, I think a hiring manager would weigh that pretty heavily."

And he has a point. The economic turmoil in recent years is a big news story, and hiring managers get that. That's why Hirsch believes that his employers weren't too bothered to hear about his impending foreclosure. They were plugged in to the news business, of course, and if *they* couldn't recognize that Hirsch was part of what society at large was going through, then we'd be even more worried about the state of the news industry than we already are. Any employer is going to be painfully aware of the economy and the effect it has had on good people.

So if your finances took a turn for the worse during the last few years due to the economy, run with it, and make that part of your story if you get to the point of discussing your credit history (more on this later). In that sense, one could argue that now is the best time in decades to have bad credit, because so many people do.

And if your finances were in tatters long before the rest of the country caught up, and you think it's more due to your own mismanagement than the rising cost of having debt, the bank bailouts, and employers being afraid to hire, well, blame your finances on the economy anyway. We won't tell.

You need a job, after all.

DISCUSSING YOUR FINANCES IN A JOB INTERVIEW

So back to that question: Should you be upfront and tell your boss that you have a lousy credit score or say nothing? After all, in so many ways, it isn't any of their business, and if it has no bearing on whether you'll do a good job, why rock the boat and bring it up?

Answer: because your credit history may come up whether you like it or not. Here are two salient items to store away in the back of your mind:

- **If you're filling out a lengthy, wordy job application, there may be some very difficult-to-notice, legalese fine print giving permission to check your credit score.** You may wind up signing permission to check your credit history and not even realize it. So that's an argument for bringing it up and explaining your situation before someone can learn about it and make a judgment without hearing your side of the story.

- **Companies often won't tell you that you were rejected because of your credit history.** So if you're thinking, "Well, I'll explain everything, if they bring it up," they may not.

Is this legal? you may wonder. Yes, unfortunately, it is—in fact, we double-checked with an employment attorney, just to make sure. Regina Jackson, an attorney at English, Lucas, Priest, and Owsley in Bowling Green, Kentucky, sent us a very informative e-mail explaining that employers can, indeed, ask you for your credit report, which you have to say in writing that they can have—and they're allowed to refuse to hire you based in part on what they find.

But if that happens, says Jackson, the employer needs to adhere to what's called the Fair Credit Reporting Act. That means—and we can only hope that businesses actually do this—they're supposed to "provide the applicant/employee with a 'pre-adverse action notification,' a copy of the individual's consumer report, and a copy of 'A Summary of Your Rights Under the Fair Credit Reporting Act.'"

Translation: They're supposed to tell you that you weren't hired due to your bad credit, and among other things, give you a copy of your credit report, so you can see what's on that report. After all, what if there are errors on the report?

What to Say, When to Say It

So should you say anything and at what stage of the interview process? That's up to you, of course. Everybody's situation is going to be different, and obviously it depends on what job you're applying for. Air traffic controller, banker, U.S. Secret Service agent, CFO—you probably better be prepared for a credit check. Graphic artist, most sales jobs, barista, TV host, photographer—you're likely in the clear. More on that in a moment.

> **Geoff:** Chris and I differ on this point, so let us each explain our view. I think, especially if there's any chance that your credit will be checked, that it's a good preemptive move to mention your financial past somewhere in the job interview. It shouldn't be the first thing out of your mouth, but I think it can be a good thing to get it out there. Yes, it may disqualify you—but your honesty may impress your future employer, too.

> **Chris:** I completely disagree. I think the strategy here should be to ace the interview, to impress them so much with your knowledge and experience that even if they do check your credit, they'll hire you anyway. After all, a credit history is just one factor of many in the hiring equation. So stop worrying about something negative that could possibly happen; go in there and light up the room with your smile and enthusiasm. That's how to get the job.

If you are going to say something, you want to be ahead of the story, and not behind it. So, for instance, if you've kept your mouth shut and your employer offers the job and adds something about all of this being contingent upon a successful background check, if you haven't spoken up, now is the time.

Don't panic—after all, this may be a moot point to your boss or hiring manager, so there's no reason to plant the idea that they should be worried. Just calmly say something along the lines of, "By the way, because I really want this job and am excited to be working here, I'd like to put this out there, in case it's important for you to know. If you're going to look at my credit history, it's taken a few hits over the last year."

Something along those lines. Calm, conversational, pleasant. If there are crickets chirping after you say that, you may want to add, "I'll be happy to explain more, if you'd like."

Your future boss may wave you off and say it's not a problem, or he or she may want to know more. Whatever you do, explain everything without hysterics, and only offer enough information to satisfy the inquiry. The more time you spend talking about it, the more likely you are to raise more questions than you answer. Keep details to a minimum, stay positive, and focus on the big picture. This is another chance to shine. If you start cursing your bank, trash talking your credit card company, or blaming your former employer, who laid you off and sent you on your journey of unemployment checks and standing in a soup line because you couldn't think of any other way to feed your kids, well, you're just going to bring a lot of drama to the table that isn't necessary. Or you might make the boss wonder, "Is he going to trash me five years from now if I lay him off?"

Better to say something like, "I got caught in the subprime mortgage meltdown like millions of others and my credit took a beating. But that's all in the past and things are looking up."

Now, this doesn't mean you can't add something about how your life has resembled Will Smith's *The Pursuit of Happyness* movie, if you think you can pull it off, and it highlights something positive about your personality. If you choose to discuss any of your personal hardships, do it in a way that your boss will believe they're hiring someone who will face a crisis in the workplace in the same way you've handled things in your own life—with class, control, and without falling apart.

But to bottom line this—say something about your credit history or don't, and then stop worrying about it. There are so many reasons an employer is going to hire or not hire you, and obsessing over your credit score is counterproductive. And remember, if two people interview you, odds are high that one of the two has a credit score worse than yours. Good luck.

Never, Never, Never Lie

The debate is whether to say anything in the interview about your credit history or not, but if a job application asks you point-blank if you've ever declared bankruptcy, the decision has been made for you. Tell the truth.

If you lie, and it's discovered during a credit check, you won't be hired. If your bankruptcy is later unearthed after you've been offered a job, you may be fired. Either way, you will have been branded a liar.

And yet, it can get "murky," admits our friendly executive search expert, Waffles Natusch. About fourteen years ago, he remembers an accountant controller who was applying for the position of CPA. The man kept debating whether to come clean that he owed child support. It had been asked on the job application, and because the Department of Child Services had told the man he had to have a job within the week or face jail, the man felt desperate. And so he lied on the application.

Two years later, Natusch spoke to him and learned that the man had been hired, and his employer had never checked to see if he owed child support. "People make their own decisions on what is right or wrong," muses Natusch, "and in his case, nobody got hurt. But in the end, he *lied*. So it's an interesting wrinkle to the idea of full disclosure."

But nobody here is endorsing lying. Remember, however you handle things, always keep in mind that one of your most precious resources is your integrity and reputation. Lose that, and you're in a really bad spot.

"While it sounds corny," concludes Natusch, "honesty is always the best policy."

CAREERS WHERE YOUR CREDIT HISTORY WILL BE A BIG ISSUE

In 2003, there was a study conducted by two organizational psychologists at Eastern Kentucky University that determined that credit checks are *not* a great way to decide if you're hiring an honest, capable employee. Incredibly—and this sounds like they came up with this just so we could throw this fact in the book—their study showed that employees with a greater number of thirty-day late payments on their credit records received, on average, higher performance ratings than workers who paid their bills on time.

Nevertheless, despite the research, there are at least two types of professions where your bankruptcy or low credit score will almost certainly torpedo your chances of being hired, in which case, we can't give you much of a pep talk. You may simply need to find a new career. Those careers are in the financial services and the federal government, especially in departments having to do with security. It's not much of a surprise, of course. When it comes to a career in money, if you're going to hire someone to manage your company's finances or advise people in how to invest their money, can you blame an employer for being reluctant to hire someone who has gone through bankruptcy?

Nothing is impossible—you may find a job if you have a mutual friend who can vouch for your character, for instance, or if you can prove that this happened because of something like being dropped by your health insurance company because your spouse had a major surgery that catapulted you into bankruptcy. But banks, investment centers, accounting firms, mortgage brokers—they're all going to be reluctant to look past your poor credit history.

Natusch is even less optimistic, saying, "If you're going to apply for a job in financial services, and you've been bankrupt, that's not going to fly—you're dead in the water."

The federal government is probably not going to hire you either. This doesn't apply to all positions, of course. You may have a good shot at convincing the Department of Agriculture that losing the fight against your $16,000 credit card debt isn't an impediment to doing a good job, but forget working at the CIA, the FBI, and anything in defense or security.

For instance, the Transportation Security Administration, which is part of the U.S. Department of Homeland Security, won't hire airport screeners or contractors who have $5,000 in overdue debt, a federal or state tax lien, or any delinquent child-support payments. They don't want any workers to be susceptible to bribes from a terrorist, which is why they'll terminate employees who develop these problems on the job.

On the upside, you probably don't want an airport screening job anyway. As a 2007 Homeland Security Department report mentioned, several TSA executives reportedly said that "the low pay [screeners] earned might be a reason why credit problems develop after hiring."

You may have a better shot at working for the government by entering law enforcement. Police stations will check your credit report, but Kim Kohlhepp, speaking on behalf of the International Association of Police Chiefs, recently told *USA Today* that the reason for those credit problems are taken into consideration. "A lot of times finances go into a tailspin as a result of a divorce," said Kohlhepp.

LOTS OF REASONS FOR OPTIMISM

By and large, plenty of good jobs are out there for people with bad credit, if you're honest about your situation and if you bring value to the company. Natusch recalls a former client, an eighty-five-year-old who was able to get past his past and find employment in the financial sector, which is even more impressive. "Five years ago," says Natusch, "a retired CFO of a hospital came to me. He had run into credit problems, had no money left, and he had to go back to work.

"I was able to help him land three short-term consulting positions with hospitals. Each one of them was losing $10 million a month, and he was able to turn all of them around. Did they care what his credit history was? No. Did they care how old he was? No. They said that if he could get them through the end of the month, they'd be happy. He could have been a Martian, and as long as he could help save their corporation, they would have been happy."

Did You Know?

Companies often use your credit report not to look at and laugh at you or feel smug about their finances (though we can't promise that doesn't happen) but to confirm your employment history and social security number.

Job-seeking Tip

"Bad credit" expert Becky Blanton suggests going into the back door of a future employer (no, not sneaking into the place through the loading dock). She suggests getting a job with a temp agency. "They're much more lax in their credit history requirements," observes Blanton. "As long as you aren't stealing and don't have any criminal activity, you can get into a company with bad credit that would normally shut you out in the average hiring process."

CHAPTER FOUR

GOOD HOUSING WITH BAD CREDIT

House poor: Describes a person who directs a large portion of his or her income to home ownership.

Dictionary.com

People can live in creative ways—and there's no better example of how than by surfing through TV channels or checking out old television series online. For instance, Jim Rockford, the detective from the 1970s series, *The Rockford Files*, lived in a mobile home, but he did so in a trailer park community on the beach. Rockford, who always seemed to be behind on bills and was once audited, clearly couldn't afford an actual house on the beach, but he probably didn't mind the cramped quarters of his trailer, because his location was so pristine.

Or think of how all of the friends on *Friends* were often rooming with each other in order to lower their rent costs. The Fonz lived in a room over a garage at the Cunninghams', which saved him money while at the same time helping out Howard Cunningham. MacGyver, Quincy, and Sonny Crockett all lived on boats. Michael Weston, the lead character in USA's *Burn Notice,* lives in a warehouse that's been converted into a home. *The Flintstones* lived in a cave, and everyone on *Gilligan's Island* lived in grass huts, and—okay, we can only take this fictional television analogy so far.

Our point is that there are a lot of types of homes out there. Some of you reading this are going to want a strictly traditional house, or at least a traditional apartment complex, and others are going to love the idea of seizing this opportunity to do something different. We're going to try to suggest ways to live just about anywhere and everywhere.

In any case, if you've come to this chapter and you're living in your parents' basement or at a hotel, when you have bad credit, finding a home in an apartment, and particularly a house, is admittedly the most time-consuming, complicated maneuver in this book. But on the plus side, once you do that, the rest of living your life with bad credit—and living it well—won't seem so difficult.

RENTING WITH BAD CREDIT

Sure, we always hear how we're throwing away money when we rent; that's the argument the housing industry gives when they try to convince people to buy homes. And we're nowhere near old enough to have experienced it yet, but we can imagine that there's something very satisfying with, thirty years after the fact, being able to say, "Ah, I've paid for this house, and it's all mine. Mine, mine, mine. Now to sell it, so I can find an assisted-living facility."

But, anyway, in this own-is-better-than-renting mentality, it's easy to forget a few important things:

- **If you rent, you're going to save a ton of cash on maintenance costs.** Need new plumbing? Does the house need a new paint job? Is there a hole in the roof? Get the landlord. You may feel like you're throwing away your rent money, but pragmatically, you're spending less money a month to rent a home than own it, and all of the extra money you'll save by renting can be put to good use in your savings account or to improve your quality of lifestyle. Oh, and if the landlord somehow refuses to fix that leaky roof? Move. Speaking of which . . .

- **If you rent, you can move.** That's the wonderful thing about renting that renters, when they start dreaming of living in a house, can easily forget. When you live in a house, especially if the market is flat, just selling your home and moving somewhere else is a long process. If you have a house, and you have bad credit, and your house is falling apart, you may find that you're somewhat stuck. There are plenty of homeowners in America who no longer have workable credit cards and can't afford to fix up their houses in order to more easily sell them. When you're a renter with or without bad credit, there's a freedom that you have—to pack up and move across the country to take a new job, for instance—that a homeowner just doesn't have.

- **There's nothing wrong with renting.** That should be obvious, but it's easy to feel like some sort of failure when you're forced to move from a house to an apartment, or if you've just never left your position as a renter. Maybe you've seen that State Farm commercial where this man finds an old, abandoned front door next to a dumpster in the city, takes it to his and his wife's dingy and darkened apartment, and then carefully sands it and paints it a bright red.

His spouse, apparently after a long, hard day, unlocks the door to their apartment and enters, looking at all of their mail, which appears to be bills. "Hey," she says, not looking up, her voice stripped of hope.

Then she sees the door leaning against their small wooden table, chuckles, and asks, "What's this?" Her husband, washing dishes, looks at her and says, "It's a promise." She looks at him, puzzled. "One day we'll have our own place." Then the voiceover says, "Being there: It's about protecting what you have and reaching for your dreams."

That's just one of a trillion or so television ads, of course. But we're always being bombarded with messages indicating that true success involves owning a house. Politicians rarely discuss renters; they talk about homeowners and the American dream. There's no escaping it—even something as innocuous as the 1947 Christmas classic *Miracle on 34th Street* has Natalie Wood's character dreaming of living in a house with a tire swing in the backyard. And, sure, living in a house is great, but popular culture would have you believe that if you rent, life is over as you know it. And it's not.

As you probably know, it can be a serious challenge to rent an apartment with bad credit. It seems crazy in a way. It's not as if you want to buy the place. You just want a place to stay. But as landlords and real estate management companies know, it can be awfully hard to move an individual or family who isn't paying their monthly rent, especially if the state or city you live in has laws stacked in favor of the tenant. If you wonder why the fuss or worry on the landlord's part, go and rent the very entertaining 1990 movie *Pacific Heights*.

Michael Keaton plays a creepy con artist who doesn't pay the rent or the security deposit to his landlords (played by Matthew Modine and Melanie Griffith) and once in his new home, he changes the locks and refuses to move.

That's not you, of course, and if your credit past is, indeed, in the past—let's say, six to twelve months—and you're starting to come away with a history of having paid your bills, you're probably going to get into an apartment just fine. But to improve the odds of getting in, you could try the following:

- **Show proof of earnings.** In Santa Monica, California, where Chris lives, there are so many folks with bad credit that the big apartment leasing companies now have a new policy. If you can show a few months' worth of bank statements that prove you're employed and that show consistent earnings, then you'll be approved. Pull some of your bank statements from the past three or four months and have them ready.

- **Be organized and prepare your paperwork.** When you fill out your rental application, staple the following paperwork to the back: four months of bank statements, a few months of pay stubs, and a letter explaining any problems that you know are on your credit history. Most people don't do this, so it's impressive when someone does.

- **Get recommendations from people.** We're not saying a letter from your mom, who may be a swell person but probably won't have a lot of pull with a landlord. However, if you have a letter vouching for your character and explaining your past situation from your employer, a bank manager, your lawyer, or maybe your former landlord, that can help.

- **Bring on a cosigner.** Since that's such an unpalatable move, we don't blame you if you reject the idea out of hand. However, your parents may be thrilled to cosign for an apartment rather than invite you into your old bedroom, which is now your father's personal man cave or your mother's scrapbooking room. Now, all of that said, some landlords won't rent to people who want to bring a cosigner. Unless you're just out of college and have little history of paying for things behind you, they may see it as a big red flag, since you're signaling from the outset that you may have trouble making your payments.

- **Money talks.** If you have it, offer a bigger security deposit—or even better, instead of a bigger security deposit, offer to pay two or three months' rent at once. And, frankly, four to six months might be what really makes it impossible for a landlord to say no. An outlay of that much cash won't be pleasant, but that's 25 to 50 percent of your year's shelter that you'll have already paid for, which may allow you to put some money aside for a rainy day, or will at least let you get ahead so that by the time you're paying your rent, you're in the swing of your new budget.

There are other things to consider, though, like an apartment locator service. Most, in fact, are free, and we think you should stay away from or use extreme caution with an apartment locator that expects you to pay for the service. Typically they make their money by collecting a fee from apartment complexes and landlords, not tenants.

Sure, in some big cities, you'll find a reputable real estate agent who may charge you for their service, but you know what? You have bad credit. You can't afford that. Go to the free apartment locator service. We're pretty adamant about that because, especially in the big cities, con artists posing as real estate agents occasionally crop up, promise that they can find a tenant an apartment for a ridiculous price, take their security deposit, and then are never seen or heard from again.

Sometimes these con artists have even managed to get away with taking the security deposit and the poor sap's first and last month's rent. One clue that you're being had: if your "broker" drives you past the apartment but doesn't take you inside because the tenants are still living in the place.

Now, granted, landlords want tenants who ideally have great or good credit scores, which is their clue that the rent will be paid on time, but the nice thing is that a good apartment location service knows what apartment complexes check FICO scores and which ones don't, and which landlords are understanding and human and who are the jerks who wouldn't rent to their own mother unless she had a 700 credit score.

So if you aren't having much luck, or just don't feel up to making a lot of calls and knocking on doors, finding an apartment locator—they're in most big cites and many smaller ones—and seeing what they can do for you is a smart decision.

Roommates with Issues

BY CHRIS BALISH

One of the scariest things you can do in the Los Angeles area is to become roommates with a stranger you met through a posting on Craigslist. There are lots of, shall we say, "unusual" people in this city, and everyone you meet has at least one roommate horror story. But since two-bedroom apartments lead to a cost savings for both roomies, many people end up moving in with complete strangers anyway.

I tried this strategy several times when I lived in St. Louis and a few more times in Los Angeles. Almost every time, on the day of the lease signing, my prospective roommate would say, "Hey, man, uh . . . do you mind putting the lease in your name? I have a few dings on my credit." I don't remember what I said in those moments, but I do remember thinking, *You waited until now to tell me this?!* In every case I agreed to sign the lease, and in every case my roommates turned out to be stellar individuals who paid the rent on time and in full. Some of them are still my best friends to this day. Back then it just surprised me how many awesome individuals had made a few mistakes that took a bite out of their credit score. Now it doesn't surprise me at all; most of my closest friends have poor credit or no credit.

BUYING A HOUSE ON BAD CREDIT

From the start, we're all led to believe that owning a house is easier than it is. There's no mortgage broker present at Barbie Malibu's Dream House, and it would have been more realistic if the three pigs had dealt with a banker instead of a wolf, although some people may not see much of a difference. But the point is, buying a house isn't child's play.

Even if you have great credit, the process isn't easy. You have to look at numerous houses with a real estate agent, and eventually you have to make an offer and maybe a counteroffer. Then there's all of that paperwork, the inspections, insurance, taxes—and let's not even get started talking about the moving van or begging your friends to help move your refrigerator. Throw in a lousy FICO score, and the process truly gets brutal.

But even with a lousy FICO score, you *can* get credit for a house and certainly for an apartment. That's the good news. The bad news is that you may not be able to buy a house right away. As Don Davis puts it, "It isn't so much the past credit history; it's the *recent* credit history." Davis is the manager of a Marysville, Washington, branch of HighTechLending, a well-regarded mortgage company in the Pacific Northwest. He adds, "A lot of people think that because they had issues a few years ago that their credit is shot. There's so much misinformation that most people just don't even try."

Okay, we should interrupt Davis right there, because obviously if you're thinking, "My past credit history isn't three years old—it's three months old!" you might think things are hopeless. They're not. We have ideas, and we'll get to those.

"Regardless of what has happened in the past," says Davis, "including bankruptcy, repossessions, and foreclosures, it is very possible to rebuild your credit in a relatively short time. Just about everyone has some kind of blip on their report, some worse than others, but it doesn't mean that it's the end of the world."

It's important to remember that how Davis describes it really is how it should be. It should be more difficult for people with a poor credit history to buy a home than someone with a stellar record. Yes, people with poor credit deserve a good place to live, and certainly their children deserve it, but part of what led millions of American families into economic trouble is the fact that they were being given the opportunity not just to buy a house, but to buy a far bigger house than they could afford.

So if you've just emerged from a financial morass—say, if you've been foreclosed on—you really should wait for a while before trying to buy a house. And if you can do that even for just a few months, it will help you in the long run, not just financially, but from a health perspective. Buying a home is stressful enough; trying to buy one right after you've lost one must be tenfold.

But let's say you can't or don't want to wait. Well, okay. Let's start looking at your options. Yep, let's go looking for a house.

FIND A FINANCIAL INSTITUTION WITH YOU IN MIND

Your bank may not be the best place to go if you have terrible credit and want a house, but a local credit union may be. Many credit unions around the country realize that millions of good people have bad credit, and they're now creating loans specifically for these people. There aren't many of them, but here are some places to consider.

- **If you live in California:** The Golden 1, the state's largest credit union, has a mortgage repair loan for people who have lost a home to foreclosure but want to buy a new one. They won't take just anyone. You have to have been employed at the same job for one year and have three years' experience in the same industry, and you can't have lost your home to foreclosure in the last two or three months. But the last six months? You're golden. It's a program designed to help people who have lost their home between six months and a year and a half ago.

- **If you live in New Jersey:** Affinity Federal Credit Union also has a program designed to help people with poor credit buy a house. The Home Loan Health Check-Up pairs the consumer with a home finance consultant who will review and compare loans to make sure they're getting the best rates available, and to offer advice on managing debt. They have another service called BASES (Budget and Score Enhancement Services) that helps their members improve their credit score and also manage debt.

- **If you live in Alabama, Missouri, Mississippi, North Carolina, and Tennessee:** The large and well-respected Lifestyle Mortgage (www.lifestyle-mortgage.com) has new home-ownership programs aimed at people with bad credit.

- **If you live anywhere in the United States, contact Lending-Tree.com:** They have a matrix of lenders across the country, and if there's a good deal out there, you'll likely find it here. Just clear away some time to deal with the phone calls and e-mails. Geoff utilized their service when he was looking for a possible way of saving his house, and he was impressed with the response. As it turned out, he didn't go with any of the lenders because he was able to work everything out with his own.

- **Check out the U.S. Department of Housing and Urban Development.** We know, we know, you hear HUD, and you think of low-income, public housing (not that there's anything wrong with that). You don't think of a tree-lined neighborhood with two-story houses and white picket fences everywhere. But you know what? Middle-class and first-time homebuyers can find a lot of great deals here, if only they'd drop by once in a while. Their website is Hud.gov, or cut to the chase and type the unwieldy http://www.hud.gov/offices/hsg/sfh/hcc/hcs.cfm into your browser. Or call 1-800-569-4287. Why go to their website? Why call? Because they have a lot of Federal Housing Administration (FHA) loans for people who have bad credit and not a ton of money to give toward a down payment. One interesting loan is the HUD 203(k) program. If you buy a house in bad need of repair—but, hey, the price is right—these loans allow you to not only buy (or refinance) the house, they'll include in the loan the cost of making the repairs and improvements. Up to $35,000 in additional money is earmarked for this purpose.

RENT-TO-OWN A HOUSE

Rent-to-own a house? Sure, it sounds suspiciously sleazy at first. As you may know—heck, maybe your credit is poor because of this—those stores that sell you rent-to-own furniture and electronics historically have been bad deals for consumers. If you make your monthly payments and eventually come to own a sofa or plasma television, you're going to come out having paid more than twice, and sometimes three times, what you would have if you had managed to put all of the money down at the outset. In other words, rent-to-own often keeps your poor credit poor, because you never have enough money to get ahead—instead, it's all going to pay for that TV, that easy chair, the kids' bunk beds, and so on. But renting-to-own a house is different.

In fact, renting-to-own is generally a better deal for the home buyer than it is the home seller, but if it's done right, everyone wins. Sellers use this option when the market isn't very good, and they don't want their house to stagnate. Buyers like you need the rent-to-own option when they can't get approval from a bank.

In the case of rent-to-own, you'll need to find a mortgage broker with experience in setting up these kinds of arrangements, which may be a little challenging. Renting-to-own a house is not a common occurrence—this is a Hail Mary pass in the real estate market—so you will have to look around, but the larger realty firms will likely have someone on staff with experience in renting-to-own homes. The real hat trick is that you need to find a seller who is willing to rent-to-own. So if you want to buy a house that hasn't been on the market very long, and the lightbulb goes over your head, and you think *rent-to-own*, just know that you'll have more trouble convincing the seller to do a rent-to-own arrangement. But if your prospective sellers complain that they're measuring the time they've had their house on the market in presidential terms, you're going to have a more receptive audience.

You'll also have to fork over a nonrefundable deposit to go toward the down payment of the house—typically 3 to 5 percent of the purchase price that is negotiated. And then, generally, you rent the house for about two years, paying monthly rent. Some (but not all) of that rent goes toward the eventual down payment of your house.

After two years, according to a typical rent-to-own contract, you now have the option to buy the home, with all of the down payment money and some of your rent money going toward the purchase price. You don't have to buy the house, but, of course, if you don't, your down payment goes down the drain. But that's part of the beauty of rent-to-own: the seller is taking a risk renting to someone who may not end up buying the house after all, but at least the seller is collecting monthly rent, and the buyer isn't locked into the house. Everyone is giving up something, and everyone's getting something, if the buyer does end up making the purchase.

And if something goes wrong with the house while you're renting, like the plumbing springs a leak or raccoons take up residence in the attic, you have the rights of a typical tenant. Your contract will probably stipulate that you're going to be the one mowing the lawn and doing the typical homeowner tasks, but if there's a leak in the roof or a flood in the basement, those are problems that are typically handled by the seller who, after all, is the landlord until you actually decide to buy and make the down payment toward your house. Still, it's ingenious in that, since you're investing in this house and you're planning on buying it, you most likely will take care of your home more so than a typical tenant.

LEASE-PURCHASE AND LEASE-OPTION

A lease-purchase is as good as buying a house. In this case, you actually sign the contract before you move in, but you won't actually purchase the property from the owner until the agreed closing date—typically one year later. The price, terms, and closing date are determined up front; all that's missing from you is a significant check, as in your down payment, which you'll pay in a year. But that doesn't mean you're living in the house for a year for free—you'll be paying the monthly mortgage. The benefit for the seller is that they can get on with their life—maybe they *have* to move to another state because someone has a job, and they want someone (that would be you) in their house making monthly payments, so they can feel free to buy another house and won't have to pay two monthly mortgages.

A lease-option is something of a combination of the rent-to-own and lease-purchase arrangement. You put down money, sometimes a lot, sometimes not so much, and sometimes it'll go toward the down payment, and sometimes it won't. It all depends on what you, the seller, and the broker work out. But you put this money down, and then you have the option later to buy the house. Usually, you lock in a price at the start of your lease-option that can bring some benefits later. If the housing market turns, and everything goes up, well, you're buying a house worth a lot for a great bargain. (Of course, the opposite can work out, where you pay more for your house than it's worth, but in that case, if you don't like that, you do have the option to jump ship.)

The whole reason for doing either a lease-purchase or a lease-option is to buy some time while you collect enough money for your down payment. If you can do a rent-to-own option, that's likely the safer route versus going with a lease-option (more time to save up your money), but not everyone is going to want to be a landlord and/or wait five years for you to sock money away into your savings account.

If you're wondering if the seller can back out of your contract, if we're talking a typical contract, the answer is "yes"—but not legally. Anything is a risk, if you don't own the house yet. The person you're buying the home from could, in theory, go bankrupt and lose the house that you've put money down on. We hate throwing that out there, because that scenario isn't common. But like crossing the street, there are risks. We don't suggest never crossing the street, but we're big believers in looking both ways and using common sense instead of impulsively rushing forward.

Of the three, lease-purchase is by far the best and most common scenario, but if you can't do that, and renting-to-own isn't a good option, a lease-option can be an excellent way to buy a house. Just make sure that you give yourself enough time to save up enough for your down payment. The last thing you want is for it to be two years into the future, and you've saved far less than what was required, and suddenly you're facing an eviction notice.

But let's not end the lease-option choice on such a downer of a note. Not only do you get more time to save up for a down payment, you get to move into your house right away—and *you've locked in your interest rate and the cost of your house.* If interest rates climb, and if the market goes up by the time you're ready to take the option to buy your house, you're going to feel like a genius.

Truly, if it works out, this is a wonderful way to get a house.

DON'T GO THROUGH
A FINANCIAL INSTITUTION AT ALL:
SELLER FINANCING

This is less common, but it's worth knowing about. In the case of seller financing, you aren't paying the bank your mortgage payment for the next fifteen or thirty years. You're paying directly to the seller, and you may even wind up with a better interest rate than you would get through a traditional lender.

On the other hand, that seller may offer you a worse interest rate. *Seller financing . . . interesting idea,* you might think. *Why don't people do this more often?*

Well, because usually you're buying a house from someone who needs to buy their own new house. The seller can't afford to wait around for thirty years for you to pay off your $200,000 (or whatever the case may be) house. They need that bank to give them $200,000 so that they can in turn buy another house, and, meanwhile, you and the bank can get to know each other for the next few decades.

But every once in a while, you find a seller who has deep pockets, or maybe someone who already has a house lined up—like the single dad with a house who plans on getting married again and moving into his new wife's digs—in which case, the owner may look at the seller-financing strategy as a good investment.

Also helpful to know: Let's say you do try to buy a house through seller financing, and the owner does want to offer you a higher interest rate to sweeten their deal. You can't blame them, especially if they don't know you. The owner sees your bad credit history and doesn't want to become part of it. (Sure, there is the argument that if a lender makes the person pay a higher interest, then that person will have more trouble paying it, so why do that to the person? We suggest that you ponder something a little simpler to grasp, like the size of the universe.)

So, anyway, your seller-financer wants to sell you their home and have you pay them directly, but wants you to pay a higher interest rate. If you crunch the numbers and feel that it's not out of the stratosphere, you can take the deal, and then once your bad credit history is pretty good, you can, theoretically, get a better interest rate from a bank, in which case you refinance, pay off the seller, and hopefully wind up with some extra money in your pocket.

Another possibility: the seller only finances part of the loan. Let's say your credit qualifies you for a $100,000 loan, but the house you want to buy costs $122,000. Well, you may be able to convince the seller to finance that last $22,000.

But all of this begs one question: Are you moving heaven and earth to get into a house that you can't really afford and, once again, find yourself cash-strapped? We want you to live well with bad credit but with the goal of eventually having good credit. We don't want you to make a move that ensures you'll be living with bad credit for the rest of your life.

HOLDING ON TO YOUR HOME

Depending on your situation, you may be reading this chapter, not because you're having any trouble finding a house right now, but because you simply want to keep what you have. If that's the case, this can be a lousy, scary time, but just remember that it's not the bad credit that will be an obstacle to finding a way to save your house—it's the lack of income coming in.

So if you have bad credit but an income, there's almost certainly a program out there that exists for you. Definitely check with your own lender, if you haven't pursued that to the nth degree. Remember: banks don't want your house. They don't want to spend the money to maintain a home, and they don't want to have to be in the position of selling a house. They just want a monthly stream of income from you.

But if things aren't going well with your own lender, check in with a trusted nonprofit like the Homeownership Preservation Foundation (www.995hope.org) or the National Foundation for Credit Card Counseling (www.nfcc.org), which, if they can't help you, will be able to divert you to a local chapter that will know if there's a housing nonprofit in your area that specializes in throwing lifelines to homeowners with bad credit.

What you want to stay away from is bringing in a third party to help you save your house—and later learn that you've hired a con artist to destroy your life. Look, you probably don't need anyone telling you this, but at the same time, homeowners are ripped off every day. According to the FBI, people are losing $6 billion every year to mortgage fraud and deed theft. So as smart as you and many people are, *somebody* is getting snookered.

What's particularly tricky is that what you hear from experts about what not to do is usually right, but not always. For instance, contrary to conventional wisdom, occasionally you can pay a company some money up front to help you negotiate with your lender, and you won't be ripped off. There are reputable firms that do this.

If you're aware of this, when a firm approaches you, it's even easier to think that, *Well,* maybe *these guys are the good guys.* But unfortunately, the crooked firms outnumber the good ones by far, so we recommend *never* paying money up front unless you simply have no problem with losing it, because even if the company is reputable, there's no guarantee that they can actually save your house. Knowing that you paid two or three thousand dollars and *still* lost your house will just drive you insane. It'd be much nicer to have that money in the bank to help you start over.

How I Almost Lost My House

BY GEOFF WILLIAMS

About three years ago, I opened a very official-looking envelope and found myself staring at a notice from the local sheriff's office. From what the letter suggested, if I wanted to stick around for it, I would soon get to see my house sold at auction.

I wasn't surprised. In fact, part of me was surprised it had taken this long. It was September. I hadn't made a house payment since March. To put it mildly, it had been a bad year. I hadn't been sick. I wasn't in the midst of some emergency preventing me from working. I was working, maybe harder than ever, but I just couldn't make enough money to pay my mortgage and utilities, put food on the table, and pay off the ever-growing pile of money that I owed Visa, MasterCard, and a personal finance company that maybe I shouldn't name since things worked out so badly between us. But more about them in a future chapter.

Anyway, the year wasn't going well, and this letter seemed to symbolize that. But I wasn't all that panicked at first. I started daydreaming about a small crowd of people standing in my front yard while a man with a gavel shouted numbers out: "One hundred fifty thousand. Nobody wants it for $150,000? Do I hear $145,000?"

I pictured high-brow society ladies lowering their spectacles, disapprovingly taking notes about our house's shortcomings, cattily mentioning that it needed a paint job, and sneering at the unkempt lawn and flattened, worn living room carpet with a couple of torn patches where Nellie, one of our dogs, chewed when she was a puppy. Frankly, I really couldn't imagine anyone wanting to buy our lived-in house, which I had bought several years earlier for $150,000, so it was hard to take the sheriff's notice seriously. But what did make an impression on me were the two people who showed up in my driveway later the same week.

They were nattily dressed, especially the reed-thin man in a blazer and tie. The blond-haired woman was plump and poised and said almost nothing, giving the sense that she might be in training. They told me that they were foreclosure specialists who could work on my behalf with my mortgage company and would be happy to get started right away.

I had no idea if these people really had the best of intentions. For all I knew, they are fine human beings, and if so, wherever they are today, I wish them well. But in part, because I knew that predatory firms thrive off the flesh of people with poor credit, I declined, telling them that I was sure I could still come up with a solution that would work for my mortgage company and myself, which was true enough. I still believed there was plenty of time.

They looked at me skeptically, but since I agreed to take their card, and that's all I would agree to, they drove away, and that was that. Or almost. At that moment, my wife and daughters, ages three and five, were arriving home from school. Seeing their faces snapped me out of my laissez-faire attitude and lit the proverbial fire that got me to work out a consolidation loan with my mortgage company, which isn't to say that I was able to do this all on my own.

After a long, tense discussion around the kitchen table on a Sunday afternoon, my mother-in-law and parents generously contributed several thousand dollars to our bank account, which I gave to my mortgage company. The rest of the money that I owed, I was able to scrounge up from the equity in my house. What saved our house was a *loan modification*. I was better off in the short run—we kept the house—but our long-term future took a slight hit. Under the new terms, we were paying about $100 more a month on our mortgage than we had been. But, again, we kept the house, and we still live here.

ALTERNATIVE HOUSING

Who says that you have to live in a house or an apartment? Or if you do live in a house, it doesn't have to be a typical two-story home with a white picket fence and garage?

Sure, that would be nice, but we're just saying that there are some other interesting possibilities that go far beyond, say, a mobile home park. Not that there's anything wrong with that, and there are some extremely fashionable trailer communities, some with swimming pools and community centers, but from a financial standpoint, we'd recommend exercising caution here: they can be awfully hard to sell for a profit. Buying a mobile home may be much cheaper than a house, but it's still an expensive proposition.

If you want a home but can't afford a typical house payment—or don't want the pressure of paying for one—there are some interesting alternatives out there, especially if you're not materialistic and don't have a large family. Keep in mind, none of these have to be permanent. You can always move on to something bigger and better later.

- **Buy a yurt.** If you know what one is, go ahead and laugh, but stay with us for a moment. Yurts are a cousin of the tent. They're portable, the frame is made with wood, and the walls are fabric. They originated with nomads who used to schlep across the lands of Central Asia, and if you don't know much about them, it's going to sound ridiculous. But yurt living is a growing movement that seems to appeal to the young and the environmentally conscious. You can generally buy a yurt for anywhere from the rock-bottom price of $5,000 to $15,000 (if you want a strong wooden floor and proper insulation). Obviously, if you want to purchase land for your yurt, that's going to be a bit more. But financing for yurts and land can be had, and it's obviously much cheaper than a house. Geoff once interviewed a yurt owner, a mom who lived in one with her baby and husband in her parents' backyard, and she seemed extremely happy. So it might be something to consider as a place to live, either permanently or temporarily. But they're not for everyone. Unless you can run a power cord out to—say, your parents' house—there is no electricity in a yurt.
- **Buy a tiny house.** And by tiny, we mean tiny. There are actually several construction companies out there, like Tiny Texas Houses in Luling, Texas, or Tumbleweed Tiny House

Company in Sebastopol, California, that specialize in building extremely small houses—as small as 64 square feet to as big as (but still tiny) 774 square feet—and can even transport them to homeowners around the country. And, yes, people are buying these homes willingly—and many of these folks probably have solid or even great credit. It's an environmental issue more than a money problem; some homeowners simply want a smaller carbon footprint. But it can be something to think about if your credit is preventing you from buying a large, expensive home. These tiny homes can cost as much as $90,000, but a more typical price is around $15,000 to $45,000. We're not suggesting you spend a dollar, however, on a tiny home, a yurt, or anything odd if you think you're going to be miserable. The point is, if you can find something that doesn't quite match up with the image of a two-story house with the white picket fence, and yet it seems like an appealing idea, why not consider it? Especially if you don't see yourself as an apartment dweller.

Couch-surfing Buddies

BY CHRIS BALISH

I recently had a longtime friend of mine visit me in California. He liked Santa Monica so much he decided to move here. So he asked if he could crash on my couch for a week until he found an apartment of his own. I said, "Sure, no problem." One week turned into two and then three, so I asked him why he hadn't found a place yet. He said, "Well, bro, all the landlords around here run credit checks and ask for references." I said, "So what's the problem?" He replied, "Wellllll . . . my credit isn't very good. In fact, it's pretty bad. And no one will rent me a place."

So what I thought would be a week or two of my friend couch surfing in my family room lasted three solid months, all because of a poor credit history. Eventually, after a little research and some teamwork, we found an awesome studio apartment for him right on the beach in Santa Monica, no credit check required. He did, however, have to pay cash every month, and pay a week early. But it worked out, and he loved his new place. And I loved having my couch back— after I had it steam-cleaned.

Still Stumped?
Even More Ideas for
Finding a Place to Live

Becky Blanton bills herself as a former journalist with almost a quarter century of experience. She is also a former homeless person. Blanton didn't set out to be homeless. In 2006 she quit her $50,000-a-year job as a small-town newspaper editor to take some time off to travel the country in her van and grieve after her abusive father died of cancer. She didn't realize it, but his death set off a wave of depression. More than a year later, she was still living out of her van, and after someone referred her to a homeless health clinic, Blanton began to recognize that her lifestyle wasn't exactly that of a glamorous travel writer. Other than her van, she was homeless. In fact, she hadn't bathed in three days.

Blanton currently ghostwrites and teaches small businesses basic Internet, blogging, and vlogging (video-blogging) skills. She can be found on the Internet at http://beckyblanton.com. Anyway, Blanton knows something about finding a home in a pinch. Not all of these ideas will be for everyone, and they go against the grain of the title and idea behind this book—living *well* with bad credit—but "well" is relative, and these might be good ideas for those who are flexible and don't feel like sleeping in a van.

- "When looking for an apartment, forget the commercial properties," advises Blanton. "Find a homeowner or someone with their own private property rental who won't run a credit check. Lots of people rent based on gut feelings or intuition about you. They're often willing to give you a break or second chance. They're also more likely to let you pay week-to-week to get started. They have flexibility that commercial leasing companies don't have."

- "Find and rent a weekly room. You can build your credit and get a good reference for a landlord in six months or less."

- "Save your money and offer to pay three months in advance. Many landlords figure if you can do that and stay caught up, you're worth taking a chance on. Then—*don't be late.*"

- "Find a live/work situation where you house-sit and/or do maintenance or yard work in exchange for part of your rent."

- "Check at your church or with people you know in close social circumstances. Many times, landlords will rent to a friend of a friend without a credit check. People will rent to someone they socialize with or know somehow without a credit check."

- "Never lie about your situation," stresses Blanton. "Be honest, and people will respond. They *want* to help. Corporations don't."

- "If you can't find a room, find a used trailer and park it in a campground," says Blanton. That, of course, is easier said than done. But if you're able to, "You'll have week-to-week or month-to-month rent payments that go down in the off-season. Some campgrounds will even pay you to live there and work part-time."

- Rent in a rundown area of town, suggests Blanton. "It's no fun to live in a bad neighborhood, but you will have a much easier time finding a place there than in a high-rent place. Live there six months, then start looking. It's easier to find a place when you have a place." That last sentiment is a good point, but still, we have to caution, if you have kids who are going to be out playing in this bad neighborhood, this is probably the absolute last move you want to make—and we hope you can come up with a different idea.

- "Sublet," suggests Blanton, and we give her big bonus points for creativity. "You will usually be dealing with a student or someone desperate to rent their place, and they'll be less inclined to worry about credit checks the closer the time is for them to have it rented." The main positive here is that you'll likely be in a good neighborhood in a college neighborhood, which can be fun and have some great resources—like the library and museums. The main negative is that your subletting will likely be quite temporary, like over the summer. Still, it's a nice stopgap while you get your future housing in order.

- "Get a roommate with good credit," suggests Blanton, "and take over the apartment when they move out. Keep paying the rent, and no one will care what your credit is."

- "Get a job working maintenance for an apartment complex," offers Blanton. "They often offer housing as part of the benefit for working for them. If you quit working for them later, you can often stay on and keep paying full rent."

- "Find a real estate agent you like and work with them, and offer to trade work for rent in some rundown properties," suggests Blanton. "Brainstorm with them. Explain that you're trying to get into a house or apartment, and your credit has hurt you. They want to rent and may work with you."

- "Contact your local social service agency. They work with landlords who are willing to rent to people with bad credit. You may have to jump through some paperwork hoops, but the apartments are usually nice and affordable. It only takes two years of good rental history to get back into the game. Don't give up, and *don't make late payments*."

READER/CUSTOMER CARE SURVEY

We care about your opinions! Please take a moment to fill out our online Reader Survey at **http://survey.hcibooks.com**.

As a **"THANK YOU"** you will receive a **VALUABLE INSTANT COUPON** towards future book purchases

as well as a **SPECIAL GIFT** available only online! Or, you may mail this card back to us.

(PLEASE PRINT IN ALL CAPS)

First Name _____ MI. _____ Last Name _____

Address _____ City _____

State _____ Zip _____ Email _____

1. Gender
- ❑ Female   ❑ Male

2. Age
- ❑ 8 or younger
- ❑ 9-12   ❑ 13-16
- ❑ 17-20   ❑ 21-30
- ❑ 31+

3. Did you receive this book as a gift?
- ❑ Yes   ❑ No

4. Annual Household Income
- ❑ under $25,000
- ❑ $25,000 - $34,999
- ❑ $35,000 - $49,999
- ❑ $50,000 - $74,999
- ❑ over $75,000

5. What are the ages of the children living in your house?
- ❑ 0 - 14   ❑ 15+

6. Marital Status
- ❑ Single
- ❑ Married
- ❑ Divorced
- ❑ Widowed

7. How did you find out about the book?
(please choose one)
- ❑ Recommendation
- ❑ Store Display
- ❑ Online
- ❑ Catalog/Mailing
- ❑ Interview/Review

8. Where do you usually buy books?
(please choose one)
- ❑ Bookstore
- ❑ Online
- ❑ Book Club/Mail Order
- ❑ Price Club (Sam's Club, Costco's, etc.)
- ❑ Retail Store (Target, Wal-Mart, etc.)

9. What subject do you enjoy reading about the most?
(please choose one)
- ❑ Parenting/Family
- ❑ Relationships
- ❑ Recovery/Addictions
- ❑ Health/Nutrition
- ❑ Christianity
- ❑ Spirituality/Inspiration
- ❑ Business Self-help
- ❑ Women's Issues
- ❑ Sports

10. What attracts you most to a book?
(please choose one)
- ❑ Title
- ❑ Cover Design
- ❑ Author
- ❑ Content

TAPE IN MIDDLE; DO NOT STAPLE

FOLD HERE

Comments

DRIVING:
BAD CREDIT IN THE
PASSENGER SEAT

IN 2002, ONE OF THIS BOOK'S two authors—Chris—was in his early thirties, feeling pretty good about where he was in life, and in many ways, his car symbolized his success. Every day, he drove his dark blue Toyota Sequoia, a $40,000 SUV, to and from work, and in his mind, the car sort of sealed his image. He was, after all, a well-coiffed news anchor for NBC in St. Louis. He had an image to maintain.

Not to mention a car. Chris could afford the $399 payment to finance his SUV. That wasn't in question. He was a news anchor, making good money.

Geoff: Care to define good money?

Chris: Sure, there's a dictionary around here.

Geoff: You know what I mean.

Chris: I'm sorry; my hearing's going out on me.

Geoff: This is print!

The problem was that Chris was spending his money about as fast as he was making it. He spent it while driving his SUV to the gym, where he had a membership. He spent it while driving to the mall to buy shoes or a new suit. He ran his plastic through the machines at the counter without thinking about it much—that is, until he paid his bills. As robust as his salary was, he could see the credit card debt creeping up, and his car payment and the rising cost of gas, frequently approaching $2 a gallon, all began to unnerve him.

If nothing else, Chris knew it wouldn't last forever. He loved St. Louis as a city, but he had Los Angeles in his sights. He knew that someday, he would pack up his car and try to take his career to the next level.

Chris decided to buy another, more affordable car, and so he put an ad in the newspaper for his SUV. He was stunned when he sold it in a matter of days to the first person who called and purchased it on the spot, giving him a cash deposit on a Friday and a cashier's check for the rest the next day. Chris hadn't even started looking for a new car.

He started panicking, wondering how he would get to work in two days, and if he should hitch a ride to the nearest car dealership. But instead, he sat down at his computer, found an easy bus route to work, and decided he would wait a little while and make his next car purchase with a lot of forethought first.

And it was then that Chris learned what we all instinctively know but can conveniently forget—it's really expensive to own a car. After a few weeks of taking the bus and enjoying being able to read the paper and work on his laptop each way, Chris suddenly realized he had about $800 extra in his checking account.

Geoff: Whoa.

Chris: Seriously. Dude, I was amazed.

It wasn't just the car payment, of course. He hadn't been paying for gas, and he had saved $130 just in parking charges. He hadn't paid for a car wash. No oil changes, no car insurance. All of the money that had been going to his SUV was suddenly back. It was so eye-opening that Chris wound up giving up the idea of buying new wheels and later wrote a book, *How to Live Well Without Owning a Car*. He still doesn't own a car.

So, yeah, there is that. You could forgo the car and save a vast amount of money on transportation, but we do recognize that what worked for Chris won't work for everyone. Geoff and his wife, much as they like the idea in spirit, can't see it working for them, and pre-sumably, a lot of people are going to feel that way. After all, there are approximately 25,000 cities, towns, villages, and suburbs in the United States, and plenty of them lack the proper public transporta-tion or even sidewalks needed to get around.

Even if you feel your family could live without a car, your spouse might fervently disagree, and living without a car on purpose could wind up being so inconvenient that it could be demoralizing to everyone involved. So if that's where you stand, we understand. If you really need to have a car, we have ideas. Some of them may actu-ally work, too.

If You're Emerging from a Bankruptcy

If you've heard that it's easier to buy a car after a bankruptcy, it's true. You will pay dearly in interest, of course. Don't kid yourself. But chances are you can buy a car. Geoff knows that from personal experience. About three months after his bankruptcy was finalized in court, he was driving his Saturn on the freeway when smoke plumes suddenly appeared out of his rear tailpipe. At least, that's what he thinks happened, as he understands how cars work, which is to say, not at all.

He managed to keep his Saturn mobile until he reached a Car-X that was about to close. Then he called home and waited for his wife and kids to pick him up. Geoff sat in the grass by the parking lot while the Car-X staff drove home. They hadn't made a diagnosis yet, but Geoff could feel it in his bones. His car, which he had bought used in 2001, had been with him for seven years. He had paid it off two years earlier. The car payment gods were calling him home.

Sure enough, the next day, Geoff learned that he was facing the expense of buying a new transmission, which would cost at least $2,000. Geoff gave Car-X his car and agreed with his wife, Susan, that they would replace the car as soon as possible, maybe in a few weeks. For now, they would drive Susan's aging Chrysler Concorde, which they had bought from Geoff's parents several years earlier for $3,000. That, at least, was paid off.

Geoff suggested not replacing the car. He reasoned with his wife that since he worked at home, they could make do. But Susan pointed out that with her occasional part-time work—she works for a nonprofit—she would need her car.

"What would happen if I weren't in the house, and the school called, and you needed to pick up one of the girls?" Susan asked. It was a good, if unlikely, question. Geoff buckled, figuring that they were debt free except for student loans and some back taxes. Work was coming in. Life was sort of good. They would buy a car.

They did, and then, of course, work stopped coming in due to what economists were calling the Great Depression 2.0.

In any case, Geoff and Susan bought a slightly used car from a Subaru dealership. The dealership found a lender that specialized in both people with bad credit and those who have emerged from bankruptcy. The interest was rotten at 29 percent, but the $430 a month was something Geoff felt he could live with, although he knew he would eventually try and refinance and get a better payment.

There is no doubt about it. If you can avoid getting a car until your credit score improves, you will be better off financially. Geoff argued this point with his wife but lost the battle. In any case, if you want a car post-bankruptcy, you'll be able to find a lender who will front you the money for your car. Why? The lender knows that after a bankruptcy, you have that clean slate. Your debts are paid off, and you're free and clear to go back into debt again. Ah, capitalism.

Of course, right about now, you might be thinking, *This is all well and good, but I need a car, and I haven't declared bankruptcy—and so I'm stuck with lousy credit, with nobody willing to lend me the money for a car. What do I do?*

Good question. It's a tough one, and we're not saying these are stellar solutions, but here are some possible answers, from the obvious to the not-so.

The Obvious: Can You Get a Hand-Me-Down Car from a Rich Relative?

We won't dwell on this for long. Provided you don't have the IQ of a chipmunk, you would have come up with this idea on your own. Just keep in mind that your parents, in-laws, grandparents, maybe your ninety-seven-year-old aunt who is giving up driving, or someone else who loves and cares for you may be planning on buying a new car, and they may be willing to give you or sell their existing vehicle to you cheap. Long shot, but possible. We're just saying.

Rent a Car—Indefinitely

One of the author's relatives has actually been renting a car every month for about eighteen months and counting. It sounds crazy at first because obviously it costs some serious jack to rent a car, but this relative has made it work for him.

The trick is that you have to find a car rental company that rewards you for renting with them repeatedly. For instance, the aforementioned relative uses Enterprise, and they have a "Month or More" program where after a couple of months of renting with them, the price per month gets significantly lower. This particular renter relative used to pay (gasp, choke) $550 a month when he began renting his car, but now he pays $425.

That's still steep, of course, but $5 cheaper than what Geoff agreed to pay for his new used car. In the last year, this particular author's relative—

Geoff: Okay, it's one of *my* relatives.

Chris: I think, by now, everyone reading this had guessed that. No offense.

Geoff: Of course not.

Anyway, in the last year, Geoff's relative has driven a slew of cars, including a Prius, a Honda, and a Chevy Cobalt. "It's kind of fun to sample a variety of different cars," admits Geoff's anonymous relative. "I don't think this is the ideal way to go, of course, but with poor credit, one's choices are limited."

But there are some benefits that make the price of renting a car month after month worth thinking about. Like, you never have to get an oil change or replace a battery. You'll never wind up at a garage or be informed that you have to pay $700 to replace some part you've never heard of because the mechanic's son is going to college soon and needs tuition money.

Plus, as Geoff's anonymous relative says, "If you have a cash flow problem, you can turn in the car anytime with no obligations." Since Geoff's relative is married and has a wife with a working car, going without a vehicle for a while is a nuisance but not a disaster.

"So while renting is more costly, there are some slim advantages, at least for me," says Geoff's relative. "I also think if someone is thinking of doing this, they might be able to score a better deal with a local, independent, nonchain car rental place."

But if the thought of renting a car indefinitely makes you queasy, you could take the next logical step.

Buy a Rental Car

In this potential scenario, you're buying a used car, so right away, you're saving money over trying to purchase a new car on bad credit, which is more than possible, but costly; and while there have been numerous drivers with a rental car, there's only one previous owner. So that's a big benefit. As the saying goes, if something goes really wrong, you know where the previous owner lives. Hertz, Avis, and Enterprise are among the companies that will sell you their rental cars.

Car Sharing

This takes the concept of carpooling to a completely new level.

Car sharing is just what it sounds like: you share a cheeseburger. (Just seeing if you were paying attention.) Now, you could share a car with your friends and family, if you were all truly organized enough, if everyone was on board with the idea, and if everyone was equally responsible with money. But those are a lot of ifs. Really, if the thought of car sharing appeals to you, you should look into joining a car-sharing organization.

Generally, it works like this: You reserve a car for a few hours, or even a few days or a week. You pay some money (obviously) to reserve the car. You go pick up the car, which may be parked at the headquarters or, just as often as not, throughout the town. So, yeah, you'll have to figure out how to get to the car you're sharing.

You drive the car during your allotted time and return it where you found it. At least with all the car-sharing sites we know of, you don't have to replace the gas you spent, and you're automatically insured when you share a car.

As for costs, there's generally a modest annual membership fee ranging from $35 to $85 a year. Then you'll pay, like, $3 to $8 an hour and 25 cents a mile, or 45 cents a mile, or more or less.

If you're already sweating, we forgot to mention that most of these car-sharing sites *give you free miles to begin with.* In Madison, Wisconsin, for instance, you'll get 150 free miles to begin with, with each reservation. So, really, these sites are trying to encourage reasonable driving—not insane, I'm-taking-a-cross-country-trip type of driving. For a short trip to pay, say, $5 an hour to use a car is not a bad deal.

Not surprisingly, when you live farther away from the East and West coasts, the less expensive car-sharing rates become. But then there are also other ways to make it less expensive. If you use the car during the off-peak hours during the dead of the night, you may pay less per hour.

Honestly, if you want to have transportation and don't need a car at your beck and call 24/7, it can be a great alternative—and you'll save a lot of money compared to what you would spend on a car payment. And a lot of these sites will bill you monthly on either your credit or debit card, so payment is a pretty streamlined process.

Some of the many car-sharing sites across the nation include:

- Zipcar.com, one of the bigger car-sharing organizations, with locations throughout America (not all states, but they're getting there), London, and two (so far) Canadian cities— Vancouver and Toronto.

- ConnectbyHertz.com—yep, Hertz, mentioned again; they're all over this.

- PhillyCarShare.com—servicing the Philadelphia area.

- CommunityCar.com—Madison, Wisconsin.

- BioCarShare.org—they share biodiesel-fueled cars in Eugene, Oregon.

- HourCar.org—the Twin Cities' answer to car sharing.

- Carsharing.net—not a site where you register to share a car, but a great site that will help you find a car-sharing organization in your area, if there is one.

As you may suspect, you're going to find car sharing easier to do if you're in a big city or a university town, where tons of college kids tend to drive (no pun intended) this sort of trend. But no matter where you live, see if it's an option. It just may be. And the great thing, too, is that you have a built-in reason to be doing this. If you don't want to tell your friends and family that you're car sharing because your credit stinks, just tell them that you're doing it for the environment.

Oh, but one more thing. These car-sharing sites aren't interested in your credit history, but they are interested in your history. That is, your driving history. If the DMV shows that you once went through a restaurant drive-through that you unexpectedly created because you ran a red light and then tried to dodge an oncoming Corvette—well, in that case, you can pretty much forget being allowed to participate in a car-sharing group.

Something to Consider

John Wilder, a fifty-nine-year-old writer and marriage coach in Jacksonville, Florida, has a ton of debt and a miserable credit score ever since his divorce several years ago. "I now buy used cars that I can pay cash for," says Wilder. "If you have money to make payments, then put it in savings. It is also a good idea to have a second backup car. This way, if you have a breakdown, and you don't have the money to fix it, then you have the backup car. This means buying older cars, but they are also cheaper for insurance, since you're only going to pay the liability."

CHAPTER SIX

STARTING A BUSINESS WITH BAD CREDIT

JOE NICASSIO, A SELF-EMPLOYED marketing guru based out of Los Angeles, was delivering a seminar not long ago, talking to a room of about forty-five professionals who had lost their jobs. "How many of you," wondered Nicassio, "had parents who told you to go to school, study hard, get a good job at a company, and that company will take care of you?"

All of the hands went up.

"Yeah?" said Nicassio, chuckling. "How's that working out for you?"

There was anxious laughter in the room. Nobody seemed slighted. After all, they were there to listen to Nicassio talk about entrepreneurship. Nicassio has been making a living on his own ever since a business disaster in his early thirties when he lost about $250,000. It is seventeen years later, and he is still paying off those debts—he figures he has 80 percent of it paid down, which would mean that he still has about $50,000 to go.

Bankruptcy, for Nicassio, is not an option. He feels that he has a moral obligation to pay those he owes. That has meant a lot of conversations with debt collectors over the years, and you can't help but wonder what must have gone through their heads when talking to Nicassio.

When times were really lean, he would send his creditors a dollar, and then on the phone, he would tell them, "We're not talking further until you thank me for the dollar I sent you. That dollar may not seem like much to you, but I moved heaven and earth to get it to you. And if you can't thank me, then you don't appreciate me."

Did the collectors thank him?

"No, not usually," admits Nicassio, who, in that case, would then hang up on them.

After his financial meltdown, Nicassio considered getting a conventional job and tried to—but due to his credit history, no employer would touch him, especially after the government told him that he owed $30,000 and put a lien on his house. Nicassio convinced the Internal Revenue Service (IRS) that the judgment was erroneous, but the government lien is still there. Nicassio says it will always be on his report.

But no matter. Nicassio will never go back to a conventional job, even if one is offered to him, and he learned a lot from that debacle. For starters, from the beginning he should have had a corporation. He does now, and because of that, he has been able to open up corporate checking accounts that are protected from creditors seeking to garnish his wages.

In any case, Nicassio has come a long way from the days when he could just afford to send his creditors a dollar at a time. A marketing guru for businesses—you can find his website at www.rapid

resultsmarketing.com—Nicassio has clients around the world, from London to Los Angeles and Hawaii to Alaska. He isn't a millionaire, of course—there's that pesky debt he is still paying off—but he is making a good living. And he, for one, can't understand why everyone isn't self-employed.

Chris: I can understand.

Geoff: It's not for everyone.

Chris: That's what I'm saying.

Geoff: But he is about to make a good point.

Chris: I agree. You shouldn't have interrupted.

Geoff: What? Me? You started—

Chris: Shhh!

As Nicassio puts it, "Everybody in this country is self-employed. If you have a job, you have one customer, and that's called putting all of your eggs in one basket. If that customer decides he doesn't like you anymore, you're screwed. But if you're self-employed and you have twenty customers and you lose one, you still have nineteen. It's almost stupid, in my opinion, to have one job. You're putting your whole fate in someone else's hands when you could have multiple customers."

And that is the point of this chapter. If you have bad credit due to a layoff, you may well be thinking that it's time to start your own business and put your destiny back in your own hands.

That said, there are two important things to think about first. For starters, if you thought it was hard to get a personal loan for yourself, wait until you find out how much fun it is to try to get a loan for a start-up business when you have a lousy credit history. In other words, you're probably going to have to find a way to start your business without a business loan. You may find one—and we'll give you some ideas—but don't count on it.

Also, no matter how glamorous the idea of working for yourself seems, you have to have the stomach for it. You've surely seen the statistics—starting a business isn't easy. If it doesn't go well, it's a sure path to poverty. But like anything, if you believe in your business, and you love working on it, you may feel that it's worth whatever comes your way—success or failure. On the other hand, it doesn't have to be all or nothing either. Ralph Hirsch is a good example of that. Remember him?

STARTING A BUSINESS TO SUPPLEMENT, NOT REPLACE, YOUR INCOME

If you see Mr. Stew's Chipotle Sauces in grocery stores, buy a bottle, will you? You'll be supporting a company that could be the poster child for beginning a business with bad credit.

Ralph Hirsch was mentioned in Chapter 3 (on job searches). During his ten months of unemployment, as he watched his bank account dwindle and kept missing his house payments, Hirsch started his own business—creating and selling a dipping sauce for chicken wings.

It may not be the most obvious thing to create, especially for a television news director, but you go where your talents lie, and Hirsch is known in his family circles for making delicious sauces. And in the midst of sending out four hundred résumés, he figured he'd better try to make money in some way.

As it turned out, Hirsch got a job before seeing his business turn into a giant success, but he made the decision to keep working at his company during the weekends and evenings. As he explains, "First, I took a massive pay cut when I accepted my current job, and if I'm going to dig myself out of this credit hole, this job isn't going to do it. We're going to have to have another source of income. Ultimately, I want this business to take off, where TV news can be my fun job and this company takes care of everything else. But there's another reason I'm building this company. After twenty-four years of being in the TV news business, I've realized that it's awfully fickle. There is no guarantee that I'll have a job tomorrow, let alone by the close of business today. So I'd better have something else I'm working on in the background to at least equal my income, if this job ever goes away."

So in the evenings, Hirsch spends time with his wife and kids, but after everyone goes to bed, he works on the paperwork aspect of his business—trading e-mails with a bottling company in Columbus or fulfilling website orders—and during the weekends, he can be found selling Mr. Stew's Chipotle Sauces at Findlay's Market, a farmer's market in downtown Cincinnati, Ohio. It isn't a booming business, but it is one—and he has been doing it with a 500 credit score.

OKAY, SIT BACK AND TAKE IN A LITTLE HISTORY . . .

If you have a credit score that's in Hirsch's neighborhood, you're going to find that credit lines are tough to get. But you'd find it tough even if you had a credit score of 760. The days of an entrepreneur of a start-up company waltzing over to a venture capitalist and wow-ing him to the point of receiving a multimillion-dollar check are a hazy memory.

But you know what? It's been tough to get credit for businesses for most of American and global history. The one recent glaring exception that a lot of people remember is back in the late 1990s leading into the twenty-first century. The Internet was really taking off, online businesses were a novelty, and investors saw dollar signs—a lot of them. So, yeah, there was this brief, glorious period when you could pretty much scrawl down an idea on a cocktail nap-kin and pass it around to some investors.

It didn't matter if the idea was all that great. Maybe you wanted to sell clothing for oysters. Chances were you'd be given millions of dollars to run a company. It sounds like we're exaggerating, and we are, but not really, not so much.

After a year or two of this, the craziest thing, of course, happened. The investors wanted to get something for their money, and a lot of these online businesses just didn't have what it takes to generate a profit. What's more (and, yes, we're generalizing), a lot of the people behind these online start-ups had invested too much money in office furniture, hiring staff, and leasing expensive offices instead of working on improving their products, their delivery service, and tin-kering with their customer service. So when times started getting worse, they didn't have enough revenue to get through a bad stretch . . . and everything just sort of began to crumble. Suddenly, a lot of businesses began going out of business: Pets.com, Furniture.com, Jewelry.com, Hardware.com . . .

But before those giddy days when venture capitalists ruled, credit was tough to come by, and since then, it hasn't been easy. Whether we're talking about the Panic of 1819, the recession in the early 1980s or early 1990s, after the dot-com bubble burst, or the terrorist attacks on September 11, 2001, there has almost always been some point when the economic picture gets bad, and yet lenders still give away money. They're more reluctant during an economic crisis, but they'll still give it away—sometimes.

Nevertheless, despite all the doom and gloom, businesses were forming during the recession of 1958 and the recession that lasted from 1973 to 1975, and companies have been created during the Great Recession. Even during the Great Depression, businesses were birthed, including Publix Super Markets, Ocean Spray Cranberries, and the Yellow Pages.

If starting your own business is a dream of yours, you can't let the absence of a credit line kill your business before you've started it. Plenty of other people with lousy credit have started their own companies—very successful ones—and you can, too. Here are some of the ways they've done it.

Find a Well-Heeled Partner

This is a popular route for a lot of entrepreneurs. If you can't get a bank to help you out, and if a venture capitalist won't pay attention to you, start sharing the details about your proposed company with your friends, family, and colleagues—it's entirely possible that you'll just be met with blank stares or lame but empty encouragement like, "Go get 'em, Tiger." But you never know. You may just find that someone likes your business idea and thinks well enough of you that they believe you can pull it off.

You shouldn't count on this though. It's a long shot at best, but it does happen. The main thing, though, is that if your partner is going to bring money to the table, you'd better have something yourself: experience. And if you don't have it—get it. Work in the industry for a while and learn everything you can about the field you want to someday own.

If you're known as a smart, capable person, and you have an extensive background working in restaurants, then opening a restaurant is a reasonable idea, and one would think your deep-pocketed uncle or best friend from college might want to become a silent partner. If you've never worked at a restaurant, but you think you have a neat concept for a restaurant, and besides, it would be cool, well, good luck finding someone to invest in that. Why should they?

Find a Well-Established Partner

Well-established, in this case, is almost the same thing as a well-heeled partner, but not quite. Instead of looking for someone with money who is willing to invest in your business, you could look for a company that is willing to work with you for a healthy share of the profits.

For instance, if you're making a food product, you might team up with a copacker. That's a company that has the facilities to process your food order, package it, label it, and possibly distribute it. What's left for you? Well, you get to pay for the materials, like the butter, eggs, and milk (let's pretend you're going to make and sell cookies), although since the copacker can buy in bulk, they'll likely purchase the ingredients for a cheaper price and then pass the savings on to you when you reimburse the copacker.

You'll also be marketing your product and lining up buyers. As you can imagine, the copacker, since they're absorbing most of the costs, will get most of the money made from the product—but you'll get a serious cut as well. The copackers are also pretty choosy, so don't expect that they'll beat down your door to work with you. It's more the other way around.

But it can work out well. Hirsch has been looking into working with a bottler for his chipotle sauces, and as he says, "There are people willing to help you. Granted, you have to pay them, but let's not get greedy. As long as you're willing to realize you're not going to do this alone, at least not starting out, then take what's out there."

He adds that the economy may have hampered the copacker or cobottler's bottom line as well, meaning, "Don't be afraid to negotiate a little. They're probably hurting a little now, too, so you can probably get them to do what you need them to do for a little less than they used to."

Microloans

Microloans is a buzzword used for loans that have been given to people in impoverished countries, and sometimes women and minority entrepreneurs in America. That said, in 1992, the Small Business Administration started their own microloan program, where they disperse money to community lending programs, with the mandate that they should give out microloans up to $35,000. The average microloan under this program is $13,000.

You should definitely look into this if you're serious about starting a company. You can go to the Small Business Administration web page (www.sba.gov) and get the information there. If you visit this website, you'll find a lengthy list of small business development centers and community investment nonprofits. Just go to the one that corresponds to the state you live in and give them a call or drop them an e-mail and see what their requirements are before they give a small business start-up owner a loan. It can't hurt to try right away and see what you need, but it's guaranteed that you'll need to show the lender a business plan, so if you don't have one, you'd better begin working on it.

Another place to check out: Kiva.org. They're based in San Francisco, and while they're mostly known for lending up to $3,000 to struggling entrepreneurs in countries around the world, they've recently begun lending up to $10,000 to some American businesses. Depending on when you contact them, they may be serving your region.

Peer-to-Peer Lending Sites

This is where regular people and deep-pocketed investors bypass, in a sense, the banks and financial firms. Peer-to-peer lending websites—LendingClub.com and Prosper.com are among the best known—offer a place for individuals to virtually meet small business owners. If these lenders think the small business owner is a good credit risk, they'll agree to loan the business money.

If this is an idea that intrigues you, a good book to add to your collection is *The Complete Idiot's Guide to Person-to-Person Lending* by Curtis E. Arnold and Beverly Blair Harzog. That said, we're not spending a lot of time on this, because getting a loan through peer-to-peer lending is becoming increasingly difficult, about as challenging as getting a traditional bank loan.

Incubators

Most cities have incubators, where you can get either free or low-cost office space, and often you'll share a receptionist, training facilities, and receive discounted (or free) electric, Internet, and phone service. You can't just waltz into these places—you'll need a business plan and a very credible idea for a company. It also helps if it's apparent that your company won't just create a paycheck for you, but that you'll be able to sooner or later hire some employees. In other words, the city wants to know: *What's in it for me?* But it really can be a terrific way to get your business going. Sometimes the incubator will split the profits, especially if you're getting everything handed to you for free. It just depends on the incubator, which you can also often find at major universities.

For more general information, the National Business Incubation Association has a website at www.nbia.org. As they'll tell you, companies that begin in incubators are four times more likely to achieve success than those who go it alone. That seems like a measurement that's kind of hard to prove one way or another, but there's little doubt that they can help.

Bartering

This can be a clever way to bring in some resources without paying for them. Now, if you're thinking about the type of bartering you learned about in elementary school, where the fur trappers bartered pelts for supplies at the general store, that is the basic idea, but, of course, it's gotten a lot more high-tech.

Catherine Mallers could tell you that. About five years ago, after she was laid off by a big wine company that was swallowed up by an even bigger wine company, Mallers knew she wanted to try and create a business of her own before her severance package of about $10,000, plus a 401(k) worth $15,000, ran out. But she needed most of her money to live on rather than sinking it into a company that might not go anywhere.

So she joined several bartering organizations—which have websites, of course—when she created the Office Grapevine, a Chicago, Illinois–based virtual office catering to busy professionals. Her company, which consists of her and several contract employees, offers transcription services, word processing, spreadsheet creation, and numerous onerous tasks that a small business might not want to do so that they can instead focus on working on their business.

Being a virtual office, Mallers's start-up costs were fairly minimal, but because she had been laid off from a wine company that had been purchased by a larger business, she was nervous about outlaying any money that she didn't necessarily have to spend. And because her father enjoyed bartering, Mallers quickly came to the conclusion that she should try the same thing.

As she lived off her severance package, she joined a local Chicago group called Art of Barter, which has a website of the same name, and another organization that no longer exists. She ultimately traded two bottles of wine worth $300 to a graphic designer who designed her website (but Mallers kicked in an extra $100, because she was so pleased with the graphic designer's work and felt the artist deserved more than the wine). For the writing on her website, Mallers hired a copywriter, who, she learned, was going on a European vacation. Mallers remembered that she had a lot of travel points from an airline. She paid a $75 transfer fee, gave the points to the copywriter, and in exchange received crisp, clear prose throughout her website.

Bartering has worked out well for her, but Mallers warns, "Just be careful. If you join a barter organization, the benefit is that you don't have to trade service for service." (In other words, you collect the resources from, say, an accountant and wait around for someone else to ask for your services.) But there are fees for these services, so Mallers says, "Know how much you can afford to pay in fees. The way they make their money is in fees. Some will charge you on the sales end and some on the payout, and some will charge you on both sides, which can get very costly very quickly."

So if your money is tight, networking among your friends, family, and professionals you meet at places like the Chamber of Commerce is probably the way to go, but some well-respected, nationally known bartering firms include BizXchange (www.bizx.com) and the International Reciprocal Trade Association (www.irta.com). Barter News.com is also an invaluable bartering resource.

Network

You knew we were going to get to that eventually, didn't you? Yep, Twitter, Facebook, and LinkedIn—these are all great websites to join to get to know people who can help you and your business. But there's a lot more out there. Still, we'll give you a quick reason why you should consider using Twitter, Facebook, and LinkedIn for your business and then move on to the groups you may not have heard of.

- **Facebook:** Usually you join here for fun. Still, if you're launching a business, if you want to get everyone's take on a new product or service you'd like your business to offer, if you want any sort of honest (hopefully honest) feedback from people who care about you (we hope), this is the place.

- **Twitter:** You sign up. You "follow" other Twitter users, and they may or may not follow you back. In the beginning, you'll be lost, but as you start adding more and more followers—and following total strangers is perfectly fine—you'll find that you can start asking questions like, "Does anyone know a good patent attorney?" Or, "I have a marketing question. Can anyone help?" Quite possibly, your followers will answer and give you the information you need. There's kind of a six degrees of separation thing working here. Just be sure to be willing to try and help others out. People in business on the Internet—granted, we're generalizing—are very big into karma.

- **LinkedIn:** You join and set up an online résumé of sorts. Tell everyone about your career and your current business, and, like Twitter, start linking to people. Unlike Twitter, you send invites to people you know, although folks break this rule all the time. LinkedIn is kind of like Facebook for serious professionals. You can update a status report, but you don't tell people you accidentally overcooked your meat loaf and the stove caught on fire. You tell people you're looking for a good accountant, or you're reading an interesting white paper, or something like that. Where LinkedIn can really help you is that you can see your contact's contacts and read all about them. If you're linked in to your ex-boss, and you notice she knows a website designer, you may want to ask your ex-boss to hook up you and that web designer.

But as we said, there are other ways to network. Some of them are pretty obvious, but if we didn't mention these, you'd wonder why on earth not. So—some other ways you can network include joining your local Chamber of Commerce. Granted, there are dues, and if you're broke, you may not want to do that yet, not if you're just starting your business. But at least drop by and tell the chamber about your burgeoning business and let them know you plan on joining one of these days, and in the meantime, could they throw any business your way? Or offer some tips on improving your business?

More organizations to consider, but again, there will be dues, include the Rotary Club International, the Lions Club International, Kiwanis (yeah, they're all still around), and Toastmasters (which is more about public speaking than anything else, but still a good networking group).

Or, if you're between the ages of eighteen and forty-one, consider checking out the Jaycees, also known as the United States Junior Chamber (www.usjaycees.org). It's a networking nonprofit that aims to help people in business development, management skills, individual training, community service, and international connections, words pretty much ripped off from their website.

GETTING FREE HELP

Who needs venture capitalists? Seriously, unless you're going to start an airport or an oil drilling company, there are a lot of ways to get what you need without spending a fortune. For instance, there's the under-the-radar, but very well-respected online organization BusinessHelpingBusiness.com.

Remember that we mentioned "karma"? Well, this website is all about that. It's free, and here's how it works: You have a need or something valuable that you believe you can give others. You go to the site. You tell people what you have, or you tell everyone what you need. You hope someone helps you out.

It's a pretty cool site. Here are a couple of sample posts directly from the website, so you can get an idea of what we're talking about:

I have a new website for kids running called *[HIDDEN TEXT]*. I'm looking for articles written by fitness professionals and track coaches that relate to kids' running and fitness. I'll credit you with your bio and link. I'm also looking for running-related sites that would like to exchange links, either with *[HIDDEN TEXT]* or *[HIDDEN TEXT]* (the wrist water bottle). Thanks!

And one more:

I am planning to launch my organic apparel online store in May '09. I would appreciate some advice from someone who has been there. I am looking to get some more info on online competitions. In addition, I am looking to market my product in a vertical approach that includes nonprofits, small/large businesses, individuals, and online communities.

Or check out the Service Corps of Retired Executives (SCORE). In case you haven't heard of SCORE, if you're really lost when it comes to starting a business, and it's definitely not knowledge that people are born understanding, this is a free nonprofit national organization made up of retired executives that may help. Their website's tagline says, "Counselors to America's Small Business," and that's just what they are.

We've heard a lot of tales from people who have used SCORE over the years, and while it doesn't always work out, it usually seems to. You're introduced to a retired executive who will mentor you and offer all the advice they can come up with as you start your business—for free. They offer in-person counseling and online counseling—both, again, for free. What could be better for a person who's starting a business and who doesn't have much money?

SCORE also offers workshops, some free and the others cheap. It's a hugely successful organization, and so, again, if you're matched with someone who can't help you, don't get discouraged. Ask to be introduced to someone else or try a different component of the group—like, try online counseling if the in-person meetings don't go well.

Another place to go: see if your community has a Small Business Development Center (SBDC). You can find out if there's a local one in the area when you're visiting the Chamber of Commerce, or go to http://www.asbdc-us.org/, type in your zip code, and see what comes up. There are about a thousand SBDCs in the country, and they all provide free advice and cheap training to established and utterly novice business owners. They're partially funded by the Small Business Administration, which means your taxes are helping to pay for the SBDC in your area. So don't feel guilty about taking up their time—go visit, tell them what type of business you hope to start, and they'll try and help you get started. "Help" being the operative word. Obviously, nobody's going to write up a business plan for you or be your assistant. But if you're looking for a road map so you can take your business down the right path, the SBDC is a fantastic place to start.

There's one other thing you might want to try if your business is starting to go somewhere—or maybe if things are going nowhere. If you live near a university with a good business school, you could contact them and ask if they do any work with start-up companies. Some business schools have formal programs where they'll have their students do market research for start-ups and even help aspiring entrepreneurs with their business plans.

But another reason to solicit free help circles right back to the issues of credit. Something that an SBDC will try to do, for instance, is help an entrepreneur access a loan. You may be eligible for some financial assistance—even if your credit score is in the toilet—and if anyone can help, it'll likely be someone at a small business development center.

THINK LEAN, THINK POSITIVE

Whatever you do, when you're starting your business and money is tight, you need to constantly be rethinking how you spend your money and—not to get all Pollyanna on you—but *you really have to have a positive attitude.* Of course, that's a message we hope you'll pick up throughout this entire book.

Not far into the Great Recession, Richard and Galit Gordon of Raleigh, North Carolina, watched in horror as attendance fell sharply at their martial arts studio. Nobody had any money, and suddenly learning tae kwon do wasn't a priority for parents who were trying to figure out how to pay for their kids' school lunches.

The Gordons were forced to shut down their business and file for bankruptcy. They could have found jobs—nothing wrong with that—or given up and become wandering hobos. Instead, they uploaded their entire tae kwon do curriculum onto their website and now offer free tae kwon do lessons online.

They make their money through Google AdSense, says Galit, "and we are looking forward to a thriving online martial arts school business—without any overhead and no need for financial assistance." None of that would have happened had the Gordons surrendered their hopes and dreams after their bankruptcy.

Hirsch possesses that never-give-up attitude as well. He says, of running a business when your personal finances are in ruins and your life seems to have collapsed around you, "It's been very hard to do, but you have to remember that the sun is going to come up tomorrow, and it's going to set tomorrow, and it doesn't matter what your credit rating is. You're still going to be alive, your kids are still going to be there, and you have to figure out how you can get through all of this. But you can do it. Maybe you won't be living your life in a 2,700-square-foot house with a swimming pool in the backyard," says Hirsch (sounding a little wistful, since that's what he used to have until pretty recently), "but even if you don't have that, is it going to matter?"

Why Your Business Loan Has Been Rejected

There are some good reasons why it's tough to get a credit line to start a business. When you're looking for a loan for yourself, you're hoping to impress the three credit issuers, which we probably all know better than the names of our own children—TransUnion, Equifax, and Experian—but when you're looking for a business loan, there are six other credit scorers out there.

And those six creditors you may want to be aware of are:

- Dun and Bradstreet (D&B): This is the most popular, well-known business credit reporting agency. Business people will typically do anything they can, short of murdering their grandma, to stay in their good graces.

- Equifax Small Business Enterprise: If the name sounds familiar, you just saw their name a few paragraphs ago—Equifax also scores credit for more than 22 million small businesses and corporations. They rank you somewhat similarly to how they do with the consumer sector; you can have a low score of 101 or a high score of 992.

- Experian Smart Business Reports: Yep, the credit issuers have really branched out. In this case, Experian won't give you a business score, but they provide evaluations of businesses' credit worthiness, which may influence a lender.

- Credit.net: This outfit has credit reports on 15 million businesses, 6 million of which have companies with four employees or less. They look at how many years you've been in business, the number of employees, public records, and stability within your industry. They grade similar to a report card, 70 to 100 percent.

- Accruint Business: This is jointly run by the Better Business Bureau and LexisNexis. They won't score you, but they can give a bank your payment history.

- Client Checker: They're pretty new, having been in this game since 2003. They look at small businesses, freelance professionals, and contractors.

- Paynet: They provide risk management tools and market insight to the commercial credit industry. Who cares? Well, they also collect real-time loan information from more than two hundred American lenders—yet another group that you want to like you.

LIVING WITH BAD CREDIT

*The only reason I made a commercial
for American Express was to pay
for my American Express bill.*

ATTRIBUTED TO ACTOR PETER USTINOV

HAVE YOU EVER THOUGHT ABOUT just how expensive it is to live? Seriously, have you ever pulled out a calculator or created a spreadsheet for life?

If you're a baby boomer, you'll get this right away, and Generation Xers will probably get it, too. But those of you born in Generation Y (we can't think of anything better to call you guys) will have to take our word for it. It is so much more expensive to live in the year 2009 than, say, 1975. And we're not just talking about standard inflation; that's an expected part of life. We're talking about all the newly created expenses that modern man (and woman) just can't live without—even though we got along fine without them just thirty years ago.

Back then you didn't have a cable or satellite TV bill. You didn't have a cell phone bill. You weren't paying a monthly fee for Internet access. You didn't pay for a Blackberry. You had no text-messaging charges. No one had an iTunes account. Satellite radio didn't exist. Tivo wasn't invented yet. No one ever heard of OnStar. And you couldn't rent movies from Blockbuster or Netflix. But thirty years later we have all those expenses and more. Each one represents another monthly expense and another way that your credit can get dinged. All of these monthly fees, which add up silently over months and years, can really take a toll on not only your checking account, but also your credit history, if you're signing up for services you ultimately can't pay for, or if the money for the services is keeping you from paying other bills, like your mortgage.

Since we're talking about how many more expenses we all have today, we might as well throw in the banks, with their web of fees, and let's not forget credit cards with their compounding interest tricks and late-payment charges. Take a look at the big picture and you can really start to see how much more expensive living has become. Small wonder that so many people get overextended and wind up having financial problems and bad credit. And get ready for even more. Every year society adopts and adapts to new technological advances and there are constantly new ways to spend money.

So if you're not willing to become Amish and you want to stay in the game and pay for Internet access, send texts, and have GPS on your cell phone, if you can't bring in more money, you're going to have to cut back somewhere. It's simple math.

And while people differ on how they spend their money, nobody's going to disagree that you should always try to get the best deal you can. So in this chapter we're going to discuss some ways to spend money despite your lack of access to credit and credit cards—and some ideas that simply might help you save money.

VACATIONS

Despite what you might think, a lousy credit history will not prevent you from going on a weekend getaway or enjoying a nice vacation with the family. Sure, a six-month dream trip around the world can be a challenge to pull off without ever using a credit card, but a one-week vacation to the islands is perfectly doable.

That said, hopefully it's clear by now that we're not advocating going off on some vacation if you're drowning in debt and can hardly put food on the table. We're saying that if your money situation is under control, or somewhat, and you want to take a vacation without credit cards, you can.

Chris: No kidding. I have two friends with completely trashed credit, and they go to Cabo San Lucas and Las Vegas all the time.

Geoff: And I've had to rent cars and stay at hotels on business trips, and for the occasional wedding out of town, and I've used a debit card. It's a bit of a hassle compared to a credit card, but not a major one.

Julie Sturgeon, who runs Curing Cold Feet, a travel agency in Indianapolis, echoes what we're saying. If you're traveling without credit cards, all you have to really do is map out a strategy in advance, make some phone calls ahead of time, be creative, and keep a good attitude.

Plan Ahead

"If you book way out in advance, that allows you to take advantage of deals and spread the payment out, so it doesn't feel like a solid chunk," says Sturgeon. "One of the cruise lines now has a program where, if you book now for cruises a year from now, they will allow you to rebook should a lower price become available."

Planning ahead, she says, also allows you to do things like—if you're leaving the country—getting a passport leisurely. If you need a passport quickly, you're going to pay a hefty rush fee. Booking vacations and airline tickets can be done online easily with a debit card—no credit required.

Do Your Research ... or Do the Opposite and Do Not Plan at All

Spend some time researching the Internet and making some phone calls. Talk to others who have used that tour operator before. Inquire if you can pay by check at booking and by cash during the trip or on board the cruise ship.

Sturgeon points out that if you don't plan ahead, you can "check out places like TravelZoo.com to see what's on sale *right now*." If your travel dates are flexible, or you wait to go on vacation until you have the cash on hand, then you're likely to find those last-minute clearance deals and save a boatload (pun intended).

Fly Southwest

"Whenever possible," laughs Sturgeon, "because they are refundable"; that is, unless you book one of Southwest's super-duper cheap "web only" fares, which may not be changeable or refundable. Southwest also has a whole section on their website offering vacation packages and last-minute deals.

What if you don't have a debit card? No problem. You can book an entire vacation package with airfare, hotel, and rental car, then mail a check or money order for the total amount to Southwest to pay for it. Call 1-800-I-FLY-SWA (435-9792) for details. The only obstacle is when you show up to rent the car. Before booking the trip ask which rental car company and location you'll pick up the car from; then call that location to see if you can rent a car without a credit or debit card. Some rental car companies allow this and some don't. It's best to call ahead to find out. But even better, don't rent a car at all on your vacation.

Start with a Travel Agent

For instance, back to our favorite travel agent, Julie Sturgeon— she says that many times a consortium of travel agencies will book blocks of cabins on various cruises, so they can buy the tickets at group rates and then pass on the group savings to individual clients. Travel agents, who get paid by the airlines, hotels, rental car companies, and such, and not by the traveler, are also going to be plugged into whatever hot deals are out there at the moment.

Speaking of cruises, Carnival Cruise Lines, for the first time ever, recently began offering cash accounts on the ship. "Cruise ships run everything on a tab," says Sturgeon, "including tips, any drinks you order poolside, incidentals and souvenirs in the gift shops, massages and spa services, shore excursions, even casino play. You hand them the door key, they swipe it, and the cost appears on your end-of-the-cruise tab total. The most widespread way to pay this expense account is to set up a credit card for it in advance." But now you can pay cash beforehand at the service desk.

As for booking air travel, a rental car, or a hotel, it will require a little more legwork if you're not paying with some sort of credit or debit card. But it is possible. Here's what you need to know.

Airplanes

Most people know that you can easily buy airline tickets with a debit card or cash card. But can you roll up to the American Airlines counter with a handful of fifty-dollar bills and walk out with a plane ticket? Yes. You can still pay for airline tickets in cash at the ticket counter, just like in the olden days. Here's how it works. First, you shop online for the best airfare and flight times. Once you know which flight you want, you call the airline on the phone, give the telephone representative the flight numbers you want, and ask to place a twenty-four-hour "courtesy hold" on your seat. The airline will give you a reservation confirmation number. Then you have either twenty-four hours or until midnight the next day to pay cash for your ticket. You will probably have to go to the airport ticket counter to pay. But if you live in a big city, many major airlines have a physical office or kiosk located somewhere downtown. Check the phone book for a closer location before you trek out to the airport.

Rental Cars

Renting a car without a credit card can be a tad tricky, but it's usually a fairly painless procedure. The main thing to know is that if you use a debit card, the rental car company may place a hold on your account in the amount of $300. So that $300 will no longer be available for withdrawal until several days after you return the car. Sometimes up to a week or more. Most rental car companies will explain this to you at the time of renting. Chris recalls seeing a few people caught off guard by this, and they had to get online to move some money around in order to make it work. If you know about it before you show up, then you can make those arrangements ahead of time.

Paying cash for a rental car can be done, but you'll have to spend some time calling around first. Not every rental car company or location will do it. Chris's friend Derek has the lowest credit score Chris has ever seen, not to mention legal trouble and pending lawsuits, but he rents cars all the time.

"I don't have a debit card, so I just pay cash," Derek says. "The rules vary from company to company, but usually they want between $300 and $500 in cash up front before they'll give you the keys. I don't mind. I figure they have to protect their interests. Just make sure you always get a receipt that clearly states you paid a cash deposit. I've never not gotten my full deposit back."

It makes sense if you think about it. With a rental car, you are taking an expensive vehicle off the lot to who knows where. So when the rental car company has access to your bank account through a debit card, they know that's a powerful incentive for you to return with their vehicle. But when you pay cash, there aren't any guarantees that you'll be back, and there are fewer ways to track you down, thus the higher security deposit.

Hotel Rooms

Credit cards are the easiest option when checking in to a hotel. Just by taking an imprint or swiping your credit card, they feel they have enough recourse if the room is damaged or if you make a two-hour call to the Vatican. If you pay with a debit card, just like the rental car companies, most hotels will implement a hold on your balance. If you expect this, it's an annoyance, but something you can probably live with. If you don't expect this, as it happened with Geoff when he took his family to a hotel one weekend so they could attend a wedding—then, well, it can cause a minor financial disaster. Call ahead and ask the front desk how much the hold is and how long before it's removed from the account.

Checking in to a hotel is one of the best places to use your low-limit, high-interest credit card if you have one. Simply give the front desk clerk your card to swipe, so there's no hold on your debit card funds, then when you check out pay the full amount in cash. That way nothing is charged to your high-interest credit card and there's no hold on your checking account that could last for days.

It's also a good idea to call the hotel a week or so in advance and ask about paying with cash. They will still likely want a card of some kind up front, but special arrangement can often be made if you make the request well in advance. Try it; you'll see. Wherever you go and whatever you do, remember that with a little research and some creativity—there's always a way to take a vacation. In fact—

Chris: Er, sorry to interrupt, but really, you don't have to rent a car on vacation. Most people spend their lives commuting or driving through traffic back and forth to the mall, so why not avoid that altogether when you're on a vacation? Go to an all-inclusive resort or stay in downtown San Francisco, Chicago, or New York, or some other cool city. Rent bikes, not cars.

Geoff: Were you run over by a car in a past life?

Chris: Don't stop me, I'm on a roll. Come on, people! You're on vacation. Pay for your vacation package up front. Then leave the driving to someone else. I do it all the time. In fact, I haven't rented a car on vacation for years.

Geoff: Okay, well, as we were saying . . .

So, anyway, weekend getaways don't have to be expensive. You can go on a road trip and camp in a state park. You could try conducting a home swap like in that movie *The Holiday* with Cameron Diaz and Kate Winslet. You could even try couch surfing.

Geoff: Okay, wait, now I have to interrupt. Couch surfing?

Chris: Yeah, couch surfing. It's a thing. Look up www.Couch Surfing.org.

Geoff: *(looks it up on the Web; thinks Chris is being irresponsible for promoting a fictional website)* Well, what do you know? You weren't joking. It's a social forum for travelers; basically, you look for people willing to let you sleep on their couch while you're traveling, and you can share your couch with wayward travelers. Interesting. Okay, back to what we were saying . . .

Or you could stay with good friends or family in exchange for letting them stay with you sometime. That saves both families the cost of an expensive hotel stay. If you're going to do a big vacation with the plane, the rental car, the hotel, and Disney World, you can at least take your trip in the off-season when packages are more reasonably priced and hotels are more willing to negotiate.

Whatever your situation, though, and whatever your budget, we hope you'll try to get away once in a while. There are a gazillion reasons to pack up and go somewhere, and a gazillion arguments not to. But living with debt can be trying at times, wearing you down emotionally and physically, so we're thinking of a vacation almost as a health issue. Besides, getting away once in a while might even help you make better financial decisions in the future. But most important, if you're working hard, even if you don't feel like you have much to show for it, you owe it to yourself to occasionally give yourself a little getaway.

HOME RENOVATIONS

Like vacations, most home improvements are expensive. But also like vacations, they don't have to be; they can always be done cheaper. That said, always assume a project will be 20 percent more than you plan for, since, if we're talking a big project, it's likely that some surprises will crop up. You should always get references for any contractor, and we like this tip from *This Old House* magazine: Never ever, ever say, "While you're at it" when talking to a contractor.

Chris: I don't get it. What's wrong with saying, "While you're at it . . . "?

Geoff: You're suddenly impulse buying—you came in with the idea to put in kitchen cabinets, but then, "while you're at it, maybe we should move the sink to this part of the house," and suddenly the $2,000 project you've hopefully budgeted for is $4,000.

Obviously, if you're a skilled do-it-yourselfer, you're going to manage the money on your projects far better than the rest of us who don't know a socket wrench from a monkey wrench. And if that's the case, you should see if there's a ReStores store near you. There are four hundred ReStores around the country, and you can find their locations at the website for Habitat for Humanity, which owns ReStores. They sell salvaged materials at half-off home-center prices. Now, unfortunately, a lot of contractors won't work with those materials, saying that they don't want to assume the liability if something goes wrong. But if you're doing the work yourself, you could save half of your costs in supplies right there.

Another way to buy cheaper supplies: building supply auctions sometimes offer some real gems for a low price. Often these items are being sold because they're slightly imperfect in some way—a small dent in a cabinet or maybe custom-made windows that weren't manufactured to the buyer's specifications—and now they're at the auction.

GARDENING

Gardening is a fun hobby that Chris thinks is for people with too much time on their hands. He may be right, but good for them because we're glad someone out there is making the planet beautiful—and while neither of us know much about gardening, we wanted to bring it up because it is a hobby that one can do on the cheap, and it can, of course, pay you back if you plant a vegetable garden.

Planting your own fruits, vegetables, and herbs is not only a cost-effective way to provide fresh food for your family, for many it is therapeutic for both body and soul.

If you live in or near a rural area, you may be able to get free manure from a local farm or ranch (horse or chicken) to fertilize your garden with, or you could also start a compost pile, which is a great way to get rid of your leftover kitchen scraps, piles of yard waste, and so on (see http://www.howtocompost.org for detailed steps on how to make a successful compost pile and what can, and cannot, be added to the pile).

But even if you're not into vegetable gardening, landscaping can be done fairly inexpensively as well. Some gardening clubs sponsor plant swaps, where you bring in flowers or plants to trade with someone else, and even if you can't find one in your area, you can always swap with your neighbors, friends, and family.

If you're an apartment dweller or you just don't have space in which to grow a garden, check out community gardening via the American Community Gardening Association (http://www.com munitygarden.org), which provides information about community gardening in the United States and Canada, or check out community supported agriculture through Local Harvest (see www.local harvest.org/csa) or the U.S. Department of Agriculture (www.nal. usda.gov/afsic/pubs/csa/csa.shtml).

And if you have a lawn service—yet another monthly or seasonal expense that homeowners have increasingly taken on—you could always give that up and tell neighbors, whether you feel this way or not, that you've decided all of those chemicals are bad for the environment, so you're going to let your grass grow au naturel.

BETTER HEALTHCARE

Health Insurance

We don't have to tell you that one of the most expensive ways to buy health insurance is as an individual. Individual plans cost more because the risk to the insurer is higher than in a group plan; group plans have more people paying premiums into the plan, so the risk is spread out over many individuals. If your employer doesn't offer health insurance, try to find group health insurance if you can. For instance, are you a member of a union? Many professional trade unions offer health insurance to their members. Chris has health insurance through his union, the American Federation of Television and Radio Artists. Are you a member of a professional organization? Many large professional groups offer group health insurance to their members.

If you can't join a group and you can't afford a conventional health insurance plan, look into a health savings account (HSA), which is the route that Geoff goes. They don't cover as much as typical health insurance, but they're better than going without a plan. Any good insurance agent can help you set up an HSA. They work like this: Every month, you put whatever money you can afford to into your HSA, and every month you pay your monthly payment to your health insurance company. The monthly payments are considerably cheaper than a typical health insurance plan, and by cheaper, if you're paying more than $1,000 a month for your family, you should be able to easily get a pretty good plan for under $500, assuming nobody covered is a smoker.

You'll be given a health savings account card—it looks like a debit card, and that's really what it is. Every time you go to the doctor or hospital, you'll pay for the services from your HSA card, which is why every month you should be socking money away. If you stay healthy, your health savings account, which you can set up through your bank or credit union, keeps growing, and because it's your money, the following year, it doesn't disappear—you still have it. And if, God forbid, you need the money in your HSA account for groceries or to pay a utility bill, you can take it out without any penalty.

Because your health savings account is part of an insurance plan, some doctors' visits—like an annual physical or a dental visit, if you have dental insurance—should be covered. And after your annual deductible (a very high one) is paid, then your insurance will pay for everything else for the remainder of the year. So you can see that this can be an effective way to spend less money and save money, if you're not going to the doctor much, and if a regular health plan isn't in the cards.

Dental Care

Dental schools and dental hygiene schools often offer free or less expensive care because you'll be worked on by dental students. That may sound like the plot to a B horror movie, but the students have an experienced dental instructor monitoring their every move. You may find that you actually get better care going to a dental school. The American Dental Association's website has a list of dental schools, so you can see if there's one in your area. Another useful website: the U.S. Department of Health and Human Services, which lists 1,200 clinics in fifty states. And DentalPlans.com is a site devoted to finding discount dental plans.

Paying Medical Bills

Health insurance companies pay less for medical services because they negotiate lower rates directly with hospitals and doctors. So if you have no health insurance, an x-ray might cost you $100; but the same x-ray is billed to your insurance plan at about half that. You can always negotiate your hospital bills yourself, of course, and there's nothing wrong with that; we've found that hospitals and doctors' offices are generally much easier to work with than credit card companies. Check out an organization called Medical Cost Advocate. They can be found on the web at MedicalCostAdvocate.com. They negotiate hospital bills before and after the procedure. So if you owe a hospital $20,000 but there's no way you can pay that much, you could hire MedicalCostAdvocate.com to negotiate for you.

You have to give your credit card or debit card information beforehand, so it's not something you do lightly, but if the payment they come up with, including their 35 percent commission, isn't less than the bill you started off with, they won't charge you anything. And because their commission is based on how much they save you, they have every incentive to lower your bill. According to their website, the typical savings are 15 to 50 percent of the original hospital bill. They do have payment plans if you can't afford to pay all at once, but they prefer the entire amount be paid right away, because that makes it easier to negotiate with the hospitals.

CEO Derek Fitteron says that Medical Cost Advocate originally started off working with small businesses and their health insurance plans, which they still do. But in the last two years, they've started using their knowledge of the healthcare industry to help the general public. If you do go it alone, though—and again, nothing wrong with that—Fitteron says step one is to carefully examine your medical bills to make sure that the procedures you owe money for were actually done. "Nine out of ten medical bills have some sort of error on them," says Fitteron.

AUCTIONS

We mentioned building supply auctions earlier in this chapter. You can, of course, buy just about anything through an auction these days, from houses to groceries. They're not always easy to find, but one of the best auction sites out there is run by the National Auctioneers Association at Auctioneers.org. If you go to "find an auction," you can click around and see what auctions are near you, and then if you can't immediately tell, you can always call them and see when their next auction is and what they're selling.

And let's not forget the eight-hundred-pound auctioneer in the room: eBay. The great thing about eBay is that you can use PayPal to buy stuff. And when we say "stuff" we mean "just about anything you can think of." The things that you can buy on eBay are truly mind-blowing. Need a solid gold spittoon for uncle Elmer's birthday present? Search eBay and you'll have ten to choose from. Looking for a pair of size 6 *Wizard of Oz* emerald shoes? You can pick from two hundred.

But let's get back to PayPal. You can open a PayPal account by making a deposit of cash from your bank account, so all of your purchases come out of that cash account. No credit card or debit card required. If you only pay cash for stuff, eBay and PayPal offer the world at your fingertips. Search it, buy it, pay for it, and four days later the UPS dude is dropping it off at your doorstep.

CONSIGNMENT SHOPS

If you don't shop at these, you don't know what you're missing. These are stores that sell slightly used, preowned but never used, and vintage clothing. Sometimes nonprofits run them; other times, they're for profit, and people will take their clothes in and sell them, picking up a few bucks in return. Then the items are marked up slightly, and the customer still gets a nice deal, because the prices are far less than what you'd pay at a department store. In particular, you can often find great baby clothes and children's clothes, since they often don't wear out as easily because kids grow right out of them.

WEBSITES WE LIKE THAT CAN HELP YOU SAVE MONEY

In no particular order, here are some sites that, if you don't know about them, may be of help:

Shopping Online

The service eBillMe.com lets you pay for a purchase from your checking account without using a credit card—or if you don't have a checking account, you can pay at a walk-in location at one of the more than 75,000 locations in the United States (alas, they don't have locations in Canada yet). They have another site, ShopDebt Free.com, that offers the same thing, powered by eBillMe.com. For the unbanked, this is a really nice deal—shop online, pay in cash, and then you get your product shipped to you.

But people who pay online through their bank might also see the appeal after listening to Samer Forzley, the vice president of marketing for eBillMe: "You don't exchange any personal financial information, none; you don't have to give that information just to buy something online."

You also aren't giving your information to eBillMe. You pay them through your online bank account—the bank sends the money to eBillMe, which sends it to the online website. They also offer a "best price guarantee," says Forzley, to all of their consumers who pay online or off. If you find the same item cheaper within ninety days, eBillMe will pay you the difference.

Paying Taxes Online

If you're self-employed, you have to pay quarterly taxes, or you may work for someone else and owe the IRS back taxes, or—well, no need to go through all of the scenarios. If you owe the IRS money, you probably know that there are a couple of sites out there that will let you pay your taxes—but those sites charge you a small but rather significant fee for sending your money to the government. If that's a beef of yours, check out Eftps.gov, which stands for Electronic Federal Tax Payment System. You have to sign up and wait a few weeks, as you give out your checking account information (another good reason to have a bank account) and wait for a pin number to be mailed to you. But once you're registered and everything is set, you can send your quarterly payments, back taxes, or whatever you owe—with no additional charge.

Coupons

Just wanted to remind everyone that there are a lot of great grocery store coupons you can find online. Some sites worth checking out include Coupons.com and RedPlum.com, for groceries; also, if you have a grocery store discount card, a lot of sites (like Shortcuts.com for Kroger and numerous other chains that they own) will let you upload coupons directly to that discount card. Procter & Gamble, aka P&G, makes a ton of products that you probably use or have used, and they, too, have a website with coupons that you can download to grocery store discount cards. Check out pgesaver.com.

And then some other nice sites that offer coupons, not necessarily for food, include BradsDeals.com and CouponCravings.com, which is run by a writer that, in the full disclosure department, Geoff has worked with at WalletPop.com, an AOL-owned personal finance blog that he writes for. He's mentioning it here not just to do a nice thing for her, but because it's a really good site.

Another thing to be aware of: every time you shop online, make sure you check to see if the product or the checkout page has a place to enter a coupon code. You can usually find this on the payment page when you're checking out; you'll see a blank field that's labeled "Enter coupon code here." There are websites that are all about furnishing coupon codes to people, so you can get discounts. One of the best: RetailMeNot.com. The codes change all the time, so just make it a habit to visit that website every time you buy online.

Dining Out

Restaurant.com is an interesting site. You can buy gift certificates to restaurants for a much cheaper price. For instance, you may find a $25 gift certificate that you can purchase for $10. Another helpful site is http://mykidseatfree.com, which will show you which restaurants let your children eat for free, and on what day and time. There are several sites like that, actually, including KidsEatFree.com and KidsMealDeals.com.

Chris: That almost makes we want to get married and have kids. Almost.

Geoff: You're not getting any younger.

Chris: Thanks for reminding me.

Free TV

If you love watching TV, you're probably all over this already. But for the rest of you, if you're fed up with your high cable or satellite television bill, why not get rid of it and watch all of your TV online? Hulu.com is probably the best and most well known site, for good reason; they offer a lot of new shows and a ton of classic television. If you have Netflix, there are a lot of movies and TV, for grownups and kids, that you can watch at the website online. You could get your news streamed in from online news sites—something to think about if cable TV isn't all that important to you. But you sports junkies, you'll probably want to keep your cable.

We know that there are hundreds of great websites like the ones above. The Internet's a big place, after all. But the point is, if you're using up a lot of brain power dwelling on all of the money you owe, think proactively and positively, too. As technology evolves and society changes, we have more and more ways to spend ourselves into oblivion—but it works both ways. If we're smart and constantly on the lookout for good opportunities, there are more ways and means than ever to help us save our money.

A Voice from the Trenches

Sherry Schroeder lives in Greater Detroit. She's forty-four, and she has had bad credit for most of her adult life. She attributes that in part to coming "from the league of the financially unconscious. My parents had no clue, their parents had no clue, and I imagine their parents before that had no clue about finances. We were poor and uneducated, living less than paycheck to paycheck because many times, no paycheck was coming into our house. My father spent what came in on beer and fishing, and my mom struggled to keep toilet paper in the house. Who had time to teach nine children about money?"

Schroeder managed to get accepted into college in England, and now a professional ghostwriter, she is married to a man who has a good job and great credit. Schroeder's own credit, however, is still in poor shape. She generously agreed to share her story of life with bad credit with us, and so here is Schroeder, in her own words:

> Surviving with bad credit ironically takes the same common sense as it does to keep your credit in good shape. I know how to have good credit. I just find creative ways not to do it. I let my heart rule my head and give out "loans" to family that I know will never be paid back. Then I am in the hole again.
>
> Once your credit is back on track, don't fall into survivor guilt. My sister often reminds me that I need to remember

where I come from financially. Then I feel terrible for reme-
dying my debt, make loans to family, incur more debt, and
the cycle starts all over again.

When you are in the throes of bad credit, you must live
to survive. We are all numbered by FICO scores, insurance
scores, and scores of debt we can't pay. Being in debt is
exhausting and some of the worst kind of stress there is.
However, it has to be managed until you can get out of
debt. It's not so bad if you are on your own. But if you have
someone to answer to in your home, you better be prepared
to be creative. This isn't a primer on creative lying. Full disclosure is always the best policy. But if there's a time when
you cannot fully disclose your financial situation, you must
always check the mail, field the calls, and pretty much be
tied to your home. It's no way to live.

But my tips for trying to live with bad credit:

- Always work out payment plans with your creditors.
  You may find your interest rates reduced and payments
  several hundred dollars off your monthly payment.

- Always pay something, even if it is just attention. Seriously.
  Don't ignore the calls. If you can't pay an agreed amount
  by the due date, call them and reschedule the date.
  Most will comply.

- Check your credit report and FICO once a year if you
  can. You are entitled to one free credit report each
  year, but not your FICO.

- Living with bad credit is doable. It simply depends on
  your comfort level. I've been homeless for a day; didn't

feel so hot. I've worked for slave wages. Then I began to educate myself. Now I am educated and still have bad credit. Why? Because it can take years to extricate yourself.

- There are tons of tricks in order to live with bad credit. You can live poorly with bad credit or you can live decently with bad credit.

- How to live poorly: don't pay anything and mooch off everyone you can.

- How to live decently: shop generic and the resale shops. Pay minimums on your credit cards and work out payment plans with those who will work with you. Don't be afraid to be a bit assertive with those who refuse to work with you. You have to be in control of your finances whether you have bad credit or not. You notice that I don't say how to live well. You can live well if you are extremely creative and your standards aren't too high. Living well is subjective.

Don't let anyone tell you that living with bad credit is easy. It's not. But it is manageable.

CHAPTER EIGHT

AVOIDING BAD CREDIT SCAMS

It's HARD TO IMAGINE WHY a con artist would go after someone who is having money problems. If your credit score is in tatters, your bank account is all but empty, and you feel like buying chewing gum is a luxury you can't afford, you might wonder why a con artist would ever bother with the likes of you. But nobody's telling that to the con artists. They've created a cottage industry in chasing after blokes who are flat broke.

Sure, thieves know they can make more money by going after the wealthy, and some enjoy robbing banks because, as career thief Willie Sutton once said, that's where the money is. But most crooks and swindlers will take anyone's cold, hard cash. And thieves know that a person with bad credit, a person who is desperate to make all of their pain go away, is usually an easy mark.

You're also a safer target than a bank or a liquor store. A thief knows that he's looking at ten to twenty years behind bars if he's caught robbing a bank. And odds are the guy behind the counter in a liquor store is wielding a gun or a baseball bat, just waiting to be crossed. In contrast to those risky endeavors, if a con artist can get you to willingly send them money, especially thousands of dollars, well, from their point of view, you're a sucker, and you deserve to lose your savings.

We want you to hang on to your money, and, of course, you do, too. But you're probably thinking that this chapter is one you're going to skip because you're too smart to fall for any swindlers. Hopefully you are. But then again, there's a reason why scams work in the first place. People invest their hard-earned money into them because, at the time, they seem like a plausible way of making a good return, or a good way to get oneself out of a bad situation. Plus, crooks work hard to envelope their scams in an aura of integrity. Maybe the company's name sounds a little like a trusted financial institution you've seen a hundred times in commercials. Or maybe what they do is perfectly legal and ethical in practice—except the person behind this scam isn't going to be legal and ethical.

The reason there's always a new scam going around is that scams work. In 2008, for instance, according to a Javelin Research study, $48 billion was lost to identity theft, which is a growing business. There were 700,000 reports of identity theft in 1999; by 2009, the number was well north of 14 million. Somebody's being fleeced.

So let's take a look at the scam hit parade. We hope you'll nod and say, "Yep, I know all of this." But scams are ever changing and always reinventing themselves. So hopefully, by taking a look at this list, if you ever come across any of these "opportunities," you won't pull out your debit card—you will run in the other direction or to the police station to file a report against these scumbags.

MORTGAGE ASSISTANCE SCAMS

As anyone who has fallen behind on their house payments and is looking for help knows, there are plenty of people offering to help you out. Not every single mortgage assistance company or program out there is a fraud, but many are. Sorting out the good guys from the bad can get pretty tricky, and yes, even the savviest homeowners can get snookered. According to FBI statistics, mortgage fraud and deed theft costs homeowners up to $6 billion every year.

So if you are behind on your mortgage, here are some guidelines to follow:

If you have found a company that promises to negotiate on your behalf with your mortgage company, and thus, while they're in these negotiations, you should be sending them money—don't. This is a common ploy. You're actually sending a criminal your mortgage payment. He or she is not negotiating on your behalf. He or she is lying to you and hoping you're going to send them another payment.

If the company asks you to sign over the mortgage while they negotiate, refuse. Then run and call the police on them. This is not a legitimate company—we don't care how legitimate they act.

If the company asks you for money up front, refuse. First, yes, there are some ethical businesses—often called third-party loss mitigation companies—that require money up front, which is what makes this so damned confusing for homeowners, and we're sorry if their business suffers because they're lumped in with the crooks and cheats. But rather than take a chance and hope you're giving money to the good guys, stay away from these companies—no matter how reputable they look.

And keep in mind, even if the company is reputable, there is no guarantee that they can actually keep the bank from foreclosing. They may try, and they may be staffed with great people who truly want to help you, but they still may fail. And you'll be out money you could have used for a hotel or other expenses.

Instead, find a nonprofit housing program that will help you work things out for free. We can't list every single one out there, but here are some examples.

- The New Jersey Housing and Mortgage Finance Agency has a pilot program (go to www.state.nj.us/dca/hmfa) that provides assistance to cover past-due mortgage payments, property taxes, water and sewer bills, and even condo association fees.

- In Ohio, the nonprofit organization Kno-Ho-Co-Ashland Community Action (http://www.knohoco.org/) can help with people who are behind on their mortgages. (The strange name does exist for a reason; it's part of the four Ohio counties they serve—Knox, Holmes, Coshocton, and Ashland.) They'll give homeowners up to $1,000 per month, for up to three months; your income has to be truly in the toilet—they're looking for people who are 200 percent under the federal poverty level.

- The state of Connecticut has two foreclosure relief programs that offer fixed-rate loans to people facing foreclosure—the Emergency Mortgage Assistance Program, or EMAP (http://www.chfa.org/firsthome/EMAP-Brochure.pdf) and the Connecticut Families program through the Connecticut Housing Finance Authority (http://www.chfa.org). This is a state that's really on the ball when it comes to foreclosing houses; they recently instituted a mandatory statewide mediation program where borrowers meet their lender in person to try to reach a settlement on a mortgage.

Most states have similar programs. They aren't everywhere, but there are many, many better alternatives at your disposal than calling a number on some junk mail that's shown up in your mailbox, promising you an end to your mortgage troubles. If you can't find or don't have the energy to search for a local nonprofit that can offer free mortgage assistance or counseling, go to your computer and log on to http://www.hopenow.com, the website for the U.S. Department of Housing and Urban Development. Or just call their toll-free number at 1-888-995-HOPE, which is staffed with HUD-approved credit counselors who can offer their expertise.

And if the first call doesn't produce the results you want, consider trying again later and trying to reach someone else. The organization is well respected and full of knowledgeable people, but you know how it is—sometimes you get the one guy on staff who hasn't been on the job as long, or you may have called when you weren't as sharp and didn't offer every bit of information you could. It's just something to keep in mind, if you're searching for advice and insight and haven't yet received any.

CAR TITLE LOANS

If you're broke, it might sound like a good idea, at first. If the bill collectors are circling, and your electric has been turned off, it sounds even better. But *do not*, absolutely *do not ever* take out a car title loan. We don't even know why these loans are legal.

This type of loan falls into the predatory lending category. Here's what happens: A lender will offer you cash, and in return you sign over the title of your paid-for car to secure the loan. Think about that for a moment. Your car, which you worked so hard to get paid off, that one debt you no longer have, is suddenly in jeopardy from the moment you agree to participate in a car title loan program. These loans are typically due in thirty days. If you don't pay the lender back in thirty days, they get the car.

What sounds so appealing is that there's generally no credit check, and the lenders typically won't push to see what your income is. They just want you to sign the title of the car over to them and pay them back or not. It doesn't matter to them. If you can pay them back, they'll be thrilled, because they're charging you triple-digit annual percentage rates. Credit cards can charge you up to 29 percent APR (the yearly cost of the loan), and that's considered ridiculously high.

Well, car title lenders often charge 250 percent APR and higher. The Consumer Federation of America has done a lot of research on this topic. One of the examples they've cited is the story of a woman who got a $3,000 loan for signing over the title of her car. She paid $400 a month to the lender. It was an interest-only payment term lasting seven months, and so it meant that after seven months, and paying $2,800, she still owed the company the original $3,000. That's the type of havoc a 250 percent interest rate can wreak on you. Yes, that $3,000 can keep the electric on, pay the mortgage company for a month or two, and buy groceries. We understand that; but keep in mind that before even a month is over, you have to make a payment and return a big chunk of that $3,000 you just borrowed.

And the following month, when your electric or mortgage is due again, and you need to buy more groceries, you'll also be worried about making a car title payment on time—and wondering if this will be the month you're going to lose your car. If anyone ever suggests you try a car title loan, *get in your car and drive away, as fast as you can.*

My Adventures in Credit Counseling

BY GEOFF WILLIAMS

Shortly after I took out a loan with Wells Fargo, cashing a check that they had sent me in the mail, I went to a credit counseling agency. It was pretty obvious to me that only a desperate fool would cash one of these checks, which seemed like a pretty good sign to me that maybe I needed help.

I had gone because one of my close friends had just started a job with the Consumer Credit Counseling Service of Atlanta, which is part of the National Foundation for Credit Counseling (NFCC), which has been around since 1951. It's a well-respected debt-counseling organization, though there's always been some understandable criticism because they're funded by the credit card industry. Still, someone has to fund a credit counseling agency, and wouldn't you rather the credit card companies foot most of the bill instead of yourself?

So after cashing this check and taking out a loan with Wells Fargo, I started doing some research on credit counseling agencies, and found one near me that I thought was part of NFCC.

It had a name, which has since changed, that was similar to the Consumer Credit Counseling Service that my friend had worked at, and it had been around for decades. To my credit, I suppose, I did manage to find a counseling service that wasn't staffed by con artists. It was an actual nonprofit.

But the way it works at an NFCC nonprofit is that if you're drowning in debt, and the collectors' calls are coming at you every few minutes, it seems, you may want to enroll in the NFCC's debt management program, or as known in the industry, a DMP. Then you pay the NFCC whatever you can afford. If that's $100 a month, that's what you pay. If you can afford $300, that's what you pay. And the NFCC staff negotiates with the credit cards, bringing down interest rates and getting the debt collectors to agree to stop calling.

For that last reason alone, I can see why some people enroll in a DMP, which is what I did, although with some outfit not associated with the NFCC. I thought that's what I was doing at the time, but, uh, no.

Incidentally, I should point out that your credit will take a hit in some way when you sign up for a debt management program. Your credit score, I've heard from various sources, won't go down, but your ability to get credit, without a doubt, will be impacted. Once you join a DMP, your accounts will be closed from you using them, and if you try to take a loan out for, say, a car, and the lender realizes your credit cards are being paid for through a debt management program—well, that doesn't help your odds of getting a loan. As one lender once told me, "Loan managers don't see this as a responsible step you're taking to get your finances under control. They see it as one step away from bankruptcy."

There is a fee for the debt management program, but hear this: Some of the unscrupulous organizations have been known to take a person's first monthly payment and keep it for themselves, letting the person fall further behind in debt. If that is what is being offered to you, absolutely refuse and leave. The average client at NFCC, according to Todd Mark, pays $18 a month. "This is regulated at the state level," says Mark, "and monthly fees shouldn't cross $50."

Fifty dollars a month is a lot, of course—$600 a year—but if your debt is significant, and if the interest rates come down far enough (and that's crucial), it could easily wind up being a bargain. And again, the average NFCC pays $18 a month. So $18 a month is $216 annually. Chances are, the NFCC, in working to bring your interest rates down, may save you $216 in interest a month.

What did I pay? That's part of the problem. I don't know. I was pretty emotional when I spoke to a counselor at my nonprofit, breaking down at one point, and by the time I came to the paperwork, I was signing my name and initials to sentences I wasn't reading but should have. All I knew as I drove away from the credit counseling service was that I felt utter relief that I was finally taking control of my debt—by having other people take control of my debt.

I paid them once a month, forking over as much as I could. Indeed, just as I hoped, slowly but surely, my credit card numbers began dropping, and the interest rates went down. But the interest rates never went down as far as I had believed they might, and my money didn't seem to be going as far as it should have. But considering all of my debts—my MasterCard, my Visa, my MBNA, my Home Depot card, my Sears card, my wife's Sears card, the Wells Fargo check, and the several hospitals we owed money to because of the cheap health insurance I had signed us up for—I assumed that I probably was having trouble tracking exactly where my money was going.

Still, slowly but surely, my bills were vanishing. When I eventually explained to my friend that I had joined this group, he sounded concerned when he informed me that they weren't part of the NFCC. That concerned me a little, too, but my credit counseling agency had a long history of being in business. They seemed perfectly reputable, and my bills were going down. The $200 that we owed on our Home Depot card went first, and then one of the hospital bills. It was slow-going, but the phone calls had long stopped, and life was good.

In fact, during my good months, when work was plentiful, I had one year where I averaged paying the nonprofit $1,000 a month. Every week, if not more, I'd study my credit card statements and could see steady progress. And yet . . . there were months when it seemed as if they weren't dropping as much as they should be, and I found it odd that despite being called a credit counseling agency, there was very little counseling going on.

I'd call the nonprofit and ask about the way my money was being handled, and I'd be told that the way the credit card's billing cycle worked, it took a while before the money I was shoveling over would make it into the credit account. I'm probably not explaining it well, but however it was explained to me, it seemed logical. And the last thing I wanted to suspect was that something wasn't right.

About four years passed with this group. That they had been giving my money to my creditors was indisputable—after four years, I only had a few credit cards left. However, one of them was a Visa with a hefty balance on it that never seemed to have changed. I understood why; I was always told that they were paying off the smaller balances first and the higher-interest loans. That is a common way to pay off bills. Nothing ominous there.

But one day, I studied one of my Visa statements, comparing the most current statement to one from a year earlier, and was stunned to see that it had gone down a total of $11. That's when I learned a good portion of my money was also going to the nonprofit, and that at my first meeting, I had signed a form stating that I agreed to "donate" a portion of my monthly payment to the organization. Maybe I was paying the $50 cap, but when I sat down and did the math, I came up with a figure quite a bit higher, calculating that I had probably paid around $3,000 to the nonprofit in four years— $3,000 that would have been very useful to bringing down my credit card debt.

I guess the lesson here is that if you join a debt management program, and I wholeheartedly endorse the idea, despite my negative experiences, you need to keep on top of what they're doing. Know exactly how much you're spending at the credit counseling agency, and exactly what they're doing for you. Don't be timid; ask for occasional sit-down meetings to go over your finances. Constantly monitor your situation to make sure you're happy with how your money is being handled.

Maybe if the $3,000 had gone toward my debt, things might have turned out differently. Or maybe if I had signed up with an NFCC-aligned credit counseling agency, or simply found a better-run organization—management and the name of the organization changed once during my tenure there—things would have worked out differently. All I know is that I left my credit counseling agency about as demoralized as when I had first come in. And, as it would turn out, I was just about a year away from filing bankruptcy.

COMPANIES THAT CATER
TO PEOPLE WITH BAD CREDIT

It's pathetic that it has to be this way, but when companies claim that "bad credit, no credit" isn't a problem, and that they specialize in working with customers with a spotty or sorry financial history, you should take a long, serious look at them before you do business.

Not that there aren't honest companies out there. In fact, if anything, we're likely to see more reputable companies than ever serving people with bad credit, because bad credit is becoming so common. So, no, don't automatically distrust every company you see that promises you good things if you have bad credit, but, nevertheless, you have to watch your step.

For instance, a couple of years ago, a company called Blue Hippo.com promoted itself as a layaway business for people with bad credit who wanted to buy computers, plasma TVs, digital camcorders, and various accessories. You'd pay them money every week, and many months later, you'd receive your computer or flat-screen TV. They may have started with good intentions, but they were fined $5 million by the Federal Trade Commission (FTC) for numerous customer service sins, like failing to tell their customers that once they started paying every week for the computer, they couldn't get any of their money back if they changed their minds, and most of all, not delivering the computers once they were paid for.

It's a shame things didn't work out better because layaway programs done right are a very responsible, cost-effective way to purchase something that you don't normally budget for. It's not as good as socking money away into an account at a credit union. But layaway is much, much cheaper than paying for something on a credit card.

Typically, a layaway program will have a small transaction fee or service charge, but otherwise, you just pay as you go, although merchants generally do have a time limit. You can't pay them here and there indefinitely, but if somehow you or the store decided things weren't working, you wouldn't lose all of your money—except for a cancellation fee. If you want to try a website layaway program, www. elayaway.com is a respected layaway company that's been around for a few years now.

Some stores have them, too, like Kmart and Sears (which are part of one company) and TJ Maxx and Marshalls (which are also owned by the same company). These stores have gained the public's trust. A new company claiming to offer a good deal to someone with bad credit may be perfectly reputable, but if you've never heard of them, you really need to look at them skeptically, especially if you're paying money before actually getting anything in return. Research them and ask friends and family what they think—or simply steer clear if there's a better, more trustworthy alternative.

IT CAN HAPPEN TO ANYONE

In the heady, more affluent days of 2003 and 2004, Robert Franklin Miller would greet his customers in an office in Washington, D.C., located only blocks from the White House. There were forty employees, darting this way and that, answering calls, typing on computers. Sporting a new suit, he took his clients into his office and had them watch a slide show that explained how his company, American Funding and Investment Corporation, was buying foreclosed homes, rehabilitating them, and then selling them to people with bad credit histories.

What nobody knew was that Miller was a con artist. He wasn't fleecing people with bad credit—he was after wealthy investors, people who you might think would have known better, although to be fair, Miller was convincing. Those forty employees, by the way?

They were victims, too. They had no idea they were just props, people Miller hired to make the company look successful.

All in all, the American Funding and Investment Corporation took in about half a million dollars before the FBI caught on to Miller's scheme, which was really just taking money and keeping it. "I just feel violated all over," a sixty-one-year-old investor, who gave Miller $3,000, told the *Washington Post* several years later.

So just remember, it can happen to anyone. You're not necessarily stupid if you fall for a con, but in order not to, you have to be skeptical and do your research. Miller, incidentally, didn't just go after the rich. He has a long history of cons. In 1992, he bilked a man out of $29,000 by pretending to be a lawyer who was willing to take on this man's criminal case. Soon after, in Annapolis, he was posing as a chiropractor, giving massages to customers in a restaurant he partially owned. He soon gave up his ownership in the restaurant, however, and then in 1994 was convicted for breaking into the restaurant and stealing food.

Seven years later, in 2001, Miller was putting ads in newspapers, promising people who had bad credit that for several thousand dollars as a down payment, he could get them into a new house. One woman, working in a convenience store, later told the *Washington Post* that she had lost $30,000 to Miller, explaining, "I was naive and excited and anxious to buy my first home. I gave this man everything I had."

And that's the tragedy of being conned when you are impoverished and struggling. It's no fun being fantastically wealthy and having your money stolen—just for starters, you may suddenly be on the fast track from being rich to becoming poor. But when you already are poor, and you're swindled out of your money, the experience is terrifying. After all, you were already financially struggling—what's next?

My Predatory Lending Story

BY GEOFF WILLIAMS

About three years into my credit counseling adventure, I learned that my wife had taken out a small loan without informing me. She was paying it back with money she was earning from a nonprofit bird rescue center that she worked at. While most of me was annoyed, I couldn't help but be relieved, too. It was only a $500 loan.

I never seemed to have a lot of options. If checks were coming in, I could stay ahead of the bills and pay the $1,200 mortgage, our $1,000 health insurance payment, and all of our other bills without too many problems. If a magazine forgot to pay me, or delayed things for a few weeks, then the problems compounded. I was always paying a credit card a few days late, it seemed.

As I looked at my wife's new loan, I couldn't quite figure out who these guys were. There was no mention of the usual players—Visa, MasterCard—but I Googled them, and they were a giant international consumer finance company, with branches throughout the United States and Canada, and with offices around the world. And as it later would become clear, once the recession kicked in and the economy started to collapse, they were making a lot of these loans to people with bad credit.

I was at once relieved and horrified that suddenly we had another lifeline to credit. I thought about canceling it right away and giving it to the credit counseling agency that I was working with, but that also felt a little crazy. After all, we had something like a $200 credit line on this new loan, if we needed it.

Of course, we wound up needing it. As the minimum payments on our credit cards kept creeping up, it was getting harder and harder to pay bills. Any savings I ever managed to accumulate were always quickly drained to pay the Visa, MasterCard, or MBNA. We had an IRA worth about $4,000 at one point, until I raided that to catch up on my mortgage.

I had talked about bankruptcy on a couple of occasions to my wife and father, both of whom thought I was crazy. But the day I asked my wife if she could request a higher credit limit from this company willing to lend her money, I could see the handwriting on the wall. When she came back to me and said that they couldn't lend her money, but they'd consider it if I cosigned with her, I knew what I was doing was madness.

But I agreed to cosign, and we went into the offices of this company, which had a branch just a few miles away from our house. We took our young girls with us; they were three and one at the time. The men who shook our hands were very polite and acted as though we were doing a grown-up, responsible thing, but I couldn't help but feel sick about the whole thing.

That said, I had borrowed money from my parents on numerous occasions over the years, and the thought of injecting $5,000 into our personal economy did wonders for my ever-sinking morale. If I could just get ahead for a little while, I kept thinking, I could pay some of these bills off and stay ahead.

For a while, that worked out fine. We made more than the monthly payments for our $5,000, and I stayed caught up on the bills. Then one day, I noticed that the company had extended our credit to $7,500, and along with our statement, the company gave us some checks we could cash, if we wanted to extend our loan.

I knew I was dealing with a company known as a predatory lender. Knowing that made me feel like I might have a chance. They thought they were going to entrap me in their web, but I wouldn't let them, I kept thinking. I kept paying down the $5,000 I owed them.

Until one day, checks from magazines weren't coming in, and our mortgage was due, and I kept looking at the checks the company had sent me, checks that I hadn't thrown away. So I'm $7,500 in debt, I later thought. At least I'm caught up on my mortgage.

To make a very long story a little shorter, the company extended our credit limit to $10,000. Then when I had trouble paying that off, they asked if I'd like to restructure the loan to make payments easier. Would I? You bet.

They could even lend me more money, they said.

And they could lend me even more, if I took out a home equity loan.

Somehow I kept resisting the notion of a home equity loan. I had been in debt long enough to know that if I did that, my story would have a very unhappy ending. But if they wanted to lend a freelance writer with a very rocky cash flow thousands of dollars, I wasn't about to question them. Besides, I had a family to feed. We restructured the loan, and I promised myself that I would get things under control.

I didn't. It probably took another year of making monthly payments and trying to pay everything down—and borrowing more money when I couldn't—to realize just how far we had come in the matter of a couple of years; that is, how far in the wrong direction we had come.

We owed the company $20,000.

BAD CREDIT: PSYCHOLOGY 101

In a suicide note, Karthik Rajaram wrote that he had considered killing only himself because of his financial troubles, but decided to take his family with him.

OPENING SENTENCE OF A *LOS ANGELES TIMES* ARTICLE,
OCTOBER 8, 2008

IT'S A TERRIBLE CATCH-22. Your money problems are keeping you up at night. You are a basket case. You need to talk to a therapist. But therapists cost money. If you spend money on a psychologist, you're going to make your problem worse while you're getting better.

Some health insurance programs pay for counseling. Frequently, health insurance is getting pretty stingy about it, but if you have health insurance, that's something to look into. If you don't, or you still can't afford what your insurance says you need to pay, you should look into what your local university or college can offer. Some campuses have programs where, for a fraction of the normal cost, you can be treated by a graduate student practicing in psychology.

Before you think, "Uh-oh," keep in mind that if it's determined you have gravely serious problems, your graduate student's professor will step in. You'll probably also find that that professor will interview you first, to see if you're a good candidate for the program. Meanwhile, you're doing a nice thing for the graduate student, and you're likely talking about your problems in a pleasant office on a nice college campus. Right there, that should put you in a pleasant frame of mind. Everyone wins.

If that doesn't interest you, your church may know where you can get some low-cost counseling. There is help out there, if you want and need it. But, first, you have to be brave enough to ask for it.

Todd Mark has been in the trenches of credit counseling for some time now and has a pretty good feel for why we spend too much. "Money," he says, "is an incredible psychological tool." Mark has been immersed in credit issues for nearly two decades now. He got his start working as a producer for Clark Howard's national radio show. (Howard, if you don't know, is a consumer advocate guru who has his own national radio show, has written some great books about managing money, and is always appearing on CNN.) Mark, who has also appeared on CNN numerous times to discuss credit, then went to work for a credit counseling nonprofit in Atlanta, until he was asked to be the vice president of education for the Consumer Credit Counseling Services of Greater Dallas, Inc. He also happens to be an old college friend of Geoff's.

"Money makes people feel powerful, especially in relationships," continues Mark. "It allows people to call the shots, telling their spouse, 'We can afford to take a vacation,' or, 'We can't take a vacation.' And, 'We can spend money on this, but we can't on that.' Money ties in with a person's feelings of success, not just with what they earn or what their credit looks like, but how you can turn money into material goods.

"And then on the flip side," continues Mark, "money can also create depression or give you a lack of self-confidence, which are also issues of power, or maybe powerlessness. Money can make people spend impulsively or recklessly because they feel down about their career, or because they're struggling with their boss at work. It can cause them to go to a bar and drink too much or go on a shopping binge and buy new shoes to make them feel better.

"People find themselves saying, 'If we have a weekend away, that'll make things better,' and so they'll spend money for a weekend that they can't afford, and then that behavior will affect your psyche, when you're thinking, 'Gee, I wish I hadn't spent that money last week because I don't have anything to eat.'

"That's an extreme example," concedes Mark, "but if your reckless spending is putting your needs into jeopardy, then that's a serious problem. So when folks are struggling with finances and bad credit, they need to be all the more acutely aware of how their emotional triggers cause them to spend or go off their budget because those are the things that throw you into chaos and keep you from achieving your financial goals."

INTO THE CHAOS . . .

It's pretty obvious what can happen if you aren't paying attention to how your money problems are affecting you psychologically. Karthik Rajaram, the fellow mentioned at the beginning of this chapter who killed his wife, sons, and mother-in-law, is an extreme example of what can happen. The papers reported that he left two suicide notes behind, and in one of them, he explained that he was "broke," losing most of his money in the stock market. Addie Polk, ninety-one, of Akron, Ohio, shot herself during an eviction about the same time. Several months earlier, a fifty-three-year-old Massachusetts woman made national headlines when on the day her house was going to be foreclosed, she faxed her mortgage company and told them she was about to kill herself. Sure enough, she carried through on her promise.

Again, these are extreme examples, but the sad tales in the newspapers are useful for the rest of us to think about, if only as a reminder of why we need to keep our wits about us. Because as you probably know, or are figuring out, there are really few experiences that can be quite as damaging to your self-esteem, although many might put divorce in the same category.

There are far worse situations than being deeply in debt, of course—seeing a loved one go through a terminal illness can suddenly make money problems seem minor—and yet what's so unique and terrible about being deeply in debt, what clearly pushes some people past the edge of rational thought, is that your self-esteem is constantly on the attack. Each phone call from a bill collector and each letter from a collection agency is a reminder that you're in the wrong, and when phone calls come repeatedly, say, every twenty minutes throughout the day, that's a lot of reminders of how wretched of a human being you are.

Even if you've become very good at looking at caller ID and ignoring the calls, the telephone ringing is still an audio reminder that things in your life have gone wrong. And if you internalize all that, think about it deeply, and lie awake nights obsessing over it, wondering how you're going to pay your debt, convinced your future is pretty much over—well, no wonder it can destroy people.

But you can't let that happen. In the end, it doesn't matter if you're stripped of your house, your car, your job, your health insurance, your TV, your computer, and all of your possessions—what matters is that you and your family are safe. If that means you're safe on a friend or family member's couch for a while, that's what it means. As long as you're still standing, you can always start over.

IT'S FUNNY HOW THE MIND WORKS

When we told Elizabeth R. Lombardi, a psychologist and physical therapist in Wexford, Pennsylvania, who is also the author of *A Happy You: Your Ultimate Prescription for Happiness,* that she would be appearing in Chapter 9, she quickly retorted:

"Really, this should be the first chapter in your book. If you think about it, you can't find a job if you're so stressed that you really can't take care of yourself. If you're going to do all of these things, like buy a house or try to buy a car, you need to get yourself in the best state that you can."

Fair point. But we're still keeping her in Chapter 9. Anyway, if you're feeling overwhelmed about your debt, keep in mind that so much of how you feel about your finances is all in your mind. Yes, the numbers are real. If you're $6,000 in debt or $60,000 in debt, you can't deny that, but just about everything else is in your mind.

- **You can't buy happiness, so stop trying:** And yet, we don't stop. Lombardi says that in the same way overeaters sometimes won't realize they're stressed until they've eaten six doughnuts, those who overspend don't always realize that they're dealing with stress by going out to the mall. "I'm not saying you can't ever go and buy a nice pair of shoes if you want to, and it makes you feel good," she says, "but you need to recognize if that's what you're doing every time you feel bad, and that there are other ways to make yourself feel better, like spending time with friends, or exercising."

- **Visualize better times ahead.** Lombardi says that you can decide that you're going to be an inspirational story. You're in the bad part, but now you can work on the good part, where eventually people look at you full of admiration for how far you've come in life.

"Life is full of ups and downs and hills and valleys," Lombardi says, "and so when you're down, it can help to remember another time when you were down, and what happened to bring you out of that. Life is always going to have those ups and downs."

BAD CREDIT AND MARRIAGE

We had planned to devote an entire chapter to marriage and bad credit. After all, there are entire books written on the topic of marriage and money. A chapter seemed like a good idea. But you know, Chris is still single, so what can he credibly say on this topic? Meanwhile, Geoff is married but feels like he is the last person who should really dispense advice. He and his wife do talk with each other about finances, and their communication skills have improved over the years, but their communicating is still a work-in-progress. And if you're a woman reading this, you may well be thinking, "No

Random Quotes on Money and Marriage

- "The big difference between sex for money and sex for free is that sex for money usually costs a lot less."

  —Brendan Behan, an Irish poet, short story writer, novelist, and playwright

- "Never marry for money. Ye'll borrow it cheaper."

  —Scottish proverb, which, depending on your point of view, may seem outdated or more relevant than ever

- "Trina! We can't afford both of us to be stupid at the same time."

  —from the short-lived sitcom *Rodney* (2002–2004). Many episodes from this affable series focused on the married couple's credit problems, which, now that we think about it, might be why the sitcom was short-lived.

way am I going to listen to marriage advice from these two jokers." Not to worry. Hoping to get some good insight into marriage and money, we turned to several authorities on the matter. For starters, we turned to Kristy L. Archuleta, a licensed marriage and family therapist (LMFT) and the director of the Financial Therapy Clinic, which opened in early 2009 at Kansas State University. It's believed to be the only financial therapy clinic in the United States. Their mission is to blend financial counseling with marriage and family therapy.

If your marriage is threatened by your debt problems, and you're lucky enough to live near Manhattan, Kansas, you can contact the clinic at the Institute of Personal Financial Planning at Kansas State University (http://www.ipfp.k-state.edu/) and ask for help. "Services at the clinic are free," says Archuleta. "Instead of asking for a financial obligation, we ask that clients participate in clinical research." In the event that their research doesn't match what the clients' needs are, Archuleta says that they'll work with the couple nonetheless.

If you live far from Kansas State University, though, you're not completely out of luck. While the clinic seems to be one-of-a-kind, Archuleta says that there are financial therapists out there, "but they are few and far between," she concedes. "Sometimes you may be able to find a marriage therapist who is willing to collaborate with a financial counselor and financial planner. The best way is to ask by word of mouth."

If you're going to go with a traditional marriage therapist, but your money problems are an overriding concern, Archuleta suggests interviewing the counselor first, "and ask about their views on how money impacts a couple's relationship and how they work with couples experiencing financial problems."

But, again, therapists do charge—they have to eat, too—so if you simply don't have any money or much to give, Archuleta points out that a lot of therapists will offer a fee based on what you earn, so don't be shy about asking if they operate on a sliding scale fee.

She adds that consumer and credit counseling agencies will provide financial counseling for a small fee. She says that some communities offer free financial counseling services through a nonprofit organization in the area, some churches will give you marital counseling, and if you work for a big company, your employer might have an employee assistance program that offers marital counseling.

"It's unfortunate," laments Archuleta. "There aren't many places to refer people to if you don't have money to spend on a therapist."

IF YOU BOTH AGREE THAT SOMETHING NEEDS TO BE DONE

Go Online

Then check out www.gottman.com, the website of John Gottman, who comes highly recommended by Maura Moore, another expert we spoke with. Moore is a psychotherapist and a licensed clinical social worker (LCSW) in northern Virginia, as well as an adjunct faculty member at the Department of Social Work at George Mason University. She's been practicing psychotherapy for about twenty years now and works a lot with married couples, and as it turns out, not surprisingly, she has seen a rise in married couples coming to her in recent years.

"Here in Virginia, the foreclosure rate is extremely high, and there are a lot of people with these upside-down mortgages, and they have to stay in relationships," observes Moore. "I'll hear, 'I'd like to divorce this SOB, but I can't afford to, because we can't split up the house, and we can't sell it, and we can't rent it.' I've seen that a lot."

Anyway, she's a fan of Gottman, who Chris mentioned earlier. Gottman has been doing research on marriage for years at the Marital Therapy Institute at the University of Washington. "His website is good to keep in touch with," says Moore, "because if you're going to try to work out these problems on your own without therapy, he has a lot of resources, and he is a prolific author, so that would be the first place I would recommend that people look."

Another website Moore recommends is www.smartmarriages.com, which she says "has a plethora of information, articles, lectures, and resources for growing healthy relationships."

Read a Book Together

Moore recommends Gottman's book *The Seven Principles for Making Marriage Work.* She also likes *The Seven Spiritual Laws of Success: A Practical Guide to the Fulfillment of Your Dreams* by Deepak Chopra. We should also mention that Moore has her own book entitled *The Simple Guide to Lasting Love.*

Here are some more titles (which should really indicate how serious a problem this is): *The Couple's Guide to Love and Money* by Jonathan Rich; *Money Before Marriage: A Financial Workbook for Engaged Couples* by Larry Burkett and Michael Taylor; and *Love, Marriage, and Money: Understanding and Achieving Financial Compatibility Before—and After—You Say "I Do"* by Alan Lavine and Gail Liberman.

Budget Together

Talk about what you're spending—every day if you have to. Moore says that some small banks and community banks—at least the one in her neighborhood—have worksheets available to help couples fill out budgets. If you're having a lot of discussions about your money, and you're both in agreement that there needs to be improvements in how you manage your finances, consider yourself lucky, because in the end, it really is all about communication.

Moore says that she saw a couple in therapy where the guy was making $150,000, and his wife had spent something like $40,000 on online shopping, just buying clothes, items at home goods stores, and so on. "It was insanity," says Moore, "and I saw his problem more as a psychological one than financial. He couldn't set boundaries for her or communicate in a way to get her to stop. She saw it in a humorous vein, as in, 'Aren't I so naughty?' Meanwhile, he's working on an ulcer. I know that women love to shop, and it's supposed to be this cutesy thing, but it's like she was sticking a knife in his gut. He's supposed to be the most important person in her life, and you know, he's not going to be able to retire when he could otherwise."

Moore suggests that if you and your spouse aren't communicating well, take a look at how you're behaving. For instance, is one person taking the parental role and the other taking the adolescent role? Moore observes that this happens sometimes, where one of the two people in a marriage spend without any real regard to the consequences. "You know, one of them acts like, 'Gee, I thought you were an ATM,'" says Moore. "So you have to frame it as, 'These are our responsibilities,' and then look at what the basic bills are and understand that paying them is a joint responsibility."

Archuleta complements that sentiment when she says that it's not just a matter of each taking responsibility, but respecting each other's financial goals. "For example, if my spouse spends too much each month, and we're constantly overextended, I lose trust, not only in his ability to make us successful financially, but I also lose part of my trust in our relationship. I may think that because he isn't responsible financially, which affects me, too, he must not value or respect me as his wife and partner. I've seen a pattern with couples when their financial behaviors differ, and they begin to discuss less and less about their financial situation.

"One ends up in the dark about the finances," continues Archuleta, "because the other doesn't want to talk about how much they have spent or how much they increased the credit card debt, because they don't want to start a fight. They lose trust and respect in their financial relationship, which leads to a loss of trust and respect in other aspects of their relationship."

She also points out—in case you want to cut your partner a little slack—that where we each came from plays a part in how we handle money. If your parents never talked about money, or if your parents did, and whether you were poor or rich—everything that went on yesterday can have an effect on how you see money today.

So all of this kind of begs a question. It's one thing if you're married and both people in the partnership agree that there is a money problem, and that it needs to be solved through better communication and planning. It's quite another if one person recognizes it and the other doesn't see it the same way. Then what?

Well, then, hang on. You may be in for a bumpy ride. Moore says you may have to start putting down ultimatums—you know, the kind where if things don't shape up in ninety days, someone ships out. And then if things get really, really bad, but divorce isn't in the cards—at least, not yet, and hopefully never—Moore puts the idea out there of postnuptial agreements. You've heard of prenuptial agreements that you sign before marriage, of course. Well, these are signed *after* a couple is married, and they're signed to help smooth over a money issue that's come up when the couple just can't agree.

Let's say that your husband has a restaurant, but it's floundering, and you're worried that someday he's going to lose everything, including your house, thanks to his business (which is really unlikely if he has a company that's incorporated). Well, you could get him to sign a postnuptial agreement stating that the house is in your name, so that if his business goes down in flames, and everything else with it, and he is sued by a ton of creditors, you'll at least know that nobody can take your home away from you.

Or maybe you're married to a lovely woman who is a shopaholic, and you're cringing because your great-aunt, who happens to be a millionaire and thinks of you as her favorite nephew, is on her deathbed. Well, if you could get your wife to agree to sign a postnuptial agreement, that inheritance would be yours and something she couldn't touch. Not that any of this is simple—it's always so easy to read something in print and quite another to actually transfer the ideas into real life—and it can all get pretty messy, and often postnuptials are, you should be warned, the beginnings of a divorce. That said, postnuptials have been known to save some marriages—and to at least protect the assets of at least half of the couple.

HOW TO COMMUNICATE

Whatever you do, you and your partner have to talk about money. You know that. Your significant other knows that. You communicated just the other day when you logged on to your bank's checking account, saw your spouse spent $48 on some new shoes or video games, and then you punched a hole in the wall. But we're talking about a little more constructive communication.

Try not to judge. That can be hard, especially if you're right, and your partner, while a terrific person, is also an idiot. But, see, strangely enough, when you articulate that your husband or wife is an idiot, they oddly take offense at that—which is why Lombardi gently suggests, "It's better to curtail your judgment and try to put forth the message, 'Okay, honey, we're on the same team. Help me understand your situation.' Once you judge that person, the walls go up."

Remind yourselves that your money problems are temporary. Hey, at least that's the goal, right? Lombardi points out that when people going on a diet miserably conclude that they can never eat pizza, they'll go out and order one and eat the whole thing. And, like dieting, if you make a mistake and do eat the whole pizza, buy the whole enchilada, or whatever metaphor you want to go with, you can start anew right away. "You each have to remind yourselves that this is a temporary state," says Lombardi, "that this isn't where you want to be, and you're going to climb up the hill together."

Make sure you have some free time, with emphasis on the "free." "If you and your partner are always talking about money, you have to get away from your home for a while and do something together where you're not discussing money. Go for a walk, cook something together, sit on the couch together—some museums have a 'free museum night.' Just make sure you spend time together and really prioritize to make sure you're not discussing finances. Otherwise, money—or the lack of money—and all the stress that goes with it can be so toxic to a relationship."

And if you notice some troubling signs in your partner, don't ignore them. Some of the signs to look for to determine if your spouse seems terribly depressed are: they've stopped sleeping, are losing (or gaining) weight, or are no longer enjoying the activities that they used to enjoy. Talk to them and try to draw them out. And don't assume everything's fine if they suddenly bounce back.

People are complicated. You might have credit problems, and maybe your husband is depressed, but it might have nothing to do with money. He might bounce back because the depression has run its course or the Cubs win a game. You may know that if you say to your wife, "Okay, honey, we're on the same team. Help me understand your situation," that she'll retort, "You've never said anything like that to me before. Are you on drugs?"

But if you get anything from this section, it should be this:

1. Try not to blame each other for your money problems; you're in this together.

2. Keep an eye out for each other.

3. Communicate about your money problems.

On that last point, think about it. Entire books have been written about marriage and money, and we guarantee that the common thread throughout all of those books is that two people can't spend money separately and expect their finances to stay together. If you hide bad news from your partner, and if he or she doesn't know what's going on with your finances, it will eventually catch up with you. And even if it doesn't, maybe you have more to worry about than just money. Seriously, if you can't share the bad times with your spouse, what kind of marriage do you have?

WHAT TO TELL THE KIDS

Don't do it; don't say anything. Let your kids enjoy their childhood. They don't need to worry about your bad credit. That's one school of thought when it comes to whether it is appropriate to share information about your money situation with your children. *Tell them. Kids are coddled enough. They need to know what's going on.* And that's another.

My Credit Card Dating Disaster

BY CHRIS BALISH

When I was living in Cincinnati I started dating this young woman whom I really liked. We were just getting to know each other and things were going well. So she asked me if I would go out to dinner with her and her mom. Meeting her mother for the first time was a little scary, but I liked this girl a lot. So I made a reservation at my favorite Italian restaurant. I'd been there many times. The dinner went well, until the check came. I had planned to pay cash for the meal because I knew my Visa card was pretty close to being over the credit limit. But in my nervous state before the dinner I forgot to go to the ATM to withdraw cash. So all I had was the Visa card. Crap! What could I do?

I literally began to sweat as my mind filled with visions of the server coming back to our table and saying my card was declined. That would go over really well with my date's mom, I'm sure. For the next ten minutes I tried to act like I was paying attention to the table conversation, but my mind was spinning. And I quite literally had sweat beading on my forehead. My date said, "Chris, are you okay? Are you feeling sick?"

Just then I saw the server coming back to our table and I cringed and braced for the embarrassment. He handed me the black foldy thing with my credit card and the bill inside and walked away. I was relieved because obviously the Visa card must have gone through. But when I opened it up, there was no bill. Instead I saw a note from the restaurant owner. It read, "Chris, I watch you on the news every morning and I know you dine here a lot. There was a problem with your card. Just stop by the restaurant tomorrow and we'll straighten it out. Thanks!"

I had to read the note three times to figure out what happened. My card was obviously declined, but the owner must have noticed that I was on a date, so he totally hooked me up and saved me from what would have otherwise been total humiliation. Disaster averted. Needless to say, I never went back to that restaurant because I didn't want to pay my bill.

Just kidding! I was there as soon as they opened the next day, and not only did I pay my bill, but I also tipped the server 40 percent— cash. I also vowed to pay down that credit card balance. It took me eighteen months, but I was determined not to let that happen to me again. That's also when I started carrying a one hundred dollar bill stashed in the lining of my wallet . . . just for emergencies.

Obviously, there is no right or wrong, no black-and-white answer here; it's just a big gloppy mess of gray. You truly may feel that your financial situation is none of your children's business, no matter how bad things get, or you might feel that you want them to know what's been going on so that they'll have realistic expectations of what your household budget can withstand. Or maybe you want to use your situation as a lesson so that someday they won't fall into the same financial traps. Or you might agree that you need to share some information with your children but at the same time think, *Boy, I had a great childhood and never had to worry about if my parents could afford things, and I'd like my kids to have the same stress-free childhood . . .*

Not surprising, "it's going to depend on the circumstances," says Susan Newman, a social psychologist whose specialty is working with children. "I don't think it's necessary to discuss your bad credit or financial problems with your kids, except in some instances. If you're going to have to move because you're losing your house, in that instance, you really do have to explain what's been happening—if this is a preteen, like a ten-year-old. These are children who have formed bonds with their friends and now you're uprooting them. You have to give an explanation, and one of the things I believe in is honesty. You can't just say to your kids that we're moving because we feel like it."

That said, be careful about going in the other direction and being completely honest and predicting that if things get really bad, maybe you'll all wind up living in a bus station. Let's not insult anyone's intelligence. Obviously, you want your kids to feel safe. If things look grim, tell them what they need to know. If they aren't that grim—you need to cancel a vacation, but you aren't losing your car—then just go with your best judgment.

Newman—and this sounds reasonable to us—says that "as long as there isn't a glaring alert that, oops, the family is in trouble, I don't believe that it's necessary to discuss bad credit with children." But if you want to talk about your bad credit in an offhanded way, where you're teaching them about credit and money, as long as you do it in a way that doesn't make your child afraid that you're all going to be losing your house and car, Newman's all for that.

"Children look up to their parents," says Newman, "and it's not a bad thing to let your child see that you've made mistakes and you're human. But I want to underscore that it depends on the child's age. I definitely wouldn't tell a six- or eight-year-old about your bad credit, or even a ten-year-old. It'll only make your child nervous and anxious."

And yet—there's nothing wrong, says Newman, with being straight with your kids that life is expensive, and your household can't always afford everything. "We parents are so intent on smoothing the path for our kids and not letting them have any bumps. We pick up the bills and cover everything, [so that] we can make life almost a fairy tale for a lot of children, where they don't have a clue about money."

At some point, your kids do need to know something about money. While a six-year-old will never really grasp the nuances of bad credit, a sixteen-year-old, who may be using their own Visa or MasterCard in the coming years, can definitely handle hearing about their parents' mistakes with money. And arguably, they should.

"I recently talked to a guy who just graduated from college," muses Newman, "and he piled on $10,000 in debt on his credit card, just from partying." If you're not playing financial advisor to your children, that could be your kid someday.

Living with Bad Credit: A Financial Snapshot

"A couple of years ago, my credit score was 805," says Shelly Wilson, a single mother who lives in a small town in Wisconsin. "Now, it's—I don't know—500-something. I find it kind of laughable. Why is a credit score so important? If you're not buying a bunch of stuff, if you don't need a car every couple of years, what difference does it make?"

Well, that *is* the point—and Wilson realizes immediately what she has said, quickly adding, "Well, if you're looking for a job, or looking for a rental, that makes a big difference." But her larger point is that every other waking moment of the day, what your credit score is has very little bearing on the rest of your life.

Wilson—at the time of this writing—isn't divorced. She is separated. After it became clear she couldn't live with her husband, who worked in the heavy equipment rental industry, Wilson left northern California for a small town in Wisconsin, where her parents and sister lived. And Wilson, who moved herself and her kids in with her sister, soon found that she was in financial hot water. Wilson didn't have a job, and with multiple sclerosis, it was harder for her to find employment.

As she puts it, "I'm not in superbad shape. I can walk and talk. I can do the basics. I just don't do it as fast. I do it a lot slower than I'd like to."

Her husband, meanwhile, was having financial problems of his own and wasn't making payments on their credit cards or on their house, and you can see where this is going. Before too long, Wilson was fielding calls from debt collectors and trying to work things out, but not getting very far. "I took this money in good faith, and I wanted to pay it back," says Wilson. "And I tried, but they'd say, 'Well, if you can pay us $200 a month. . . .' and I'd say, 'I can't because I have five other credit cards.'"

Wilson says there were screaming fights with some of the debt collectors on the phone. "They pushed my buttons. They didn't have a clue—they didn't know what I had gone through—and they didn't care, and why should they? They were doing their job, and I understood that."

She sought help with a credit counseling service and vividly remembers the counselor saying, "You realize your debt is $1,000 dollars more a month than what your income is?" Wilson contacted her husband and advised him that she was declaring bankruptcy. Living in the long shadow of bankruptcy has been a challenge for Wilson, who lives on disability and a small paycheck she receives for working three hours a day at a day care at an elementary school. But she has managed to find an apartment, land her day care job, and slowly put the pieces of her life back together despite her credit score.

A lot of how she did it had to do with the luck of living in a small town, perhaps, where everyone knows everyone's business, and that Wilson was honest about her situation with everyone she encountered. She got her apartment because she learned that someone she knew had a daughter who was moving out. And so Wilson talked to both her friend's daughter and the landlord, who ended the conversation by saying, "I'm not going to be doing a credit check; I trust you."

She wound up taking over her sister's job at the day care. But she also told her employer about her situation, and because of this, she was willing to give Wilson the benefit of the doubt. In fact, being honest about her situation has helped in immeasurable ways. When Wilson agreed to let her six-year-old daughter join the Girl Scouts, she quickly learned about the $12 registration fee. She was asked if it would be a problem to pay it, and Wilson stammered, mulling it over, and then admitted, "It seems so lame, but we live on a fixed income, and if it can be waived, I would appreciate that."

The troop leader then found several other fees that could be waived, leaving Wilson to now marvel: "That would have broken the bank if I hadn't sucked up my pride and admitted that I needed help." And then Wilson decided to be an adult volunteer for her daughter's troop, reasoning that if she couldn't pay the fees, she could at least help the organization out in that way. "And realizing that the Girl Scouts need this help, that it's not all about the money," she says, "made me feel a lot better."

My Decision to Declare Bankruptcy

BY GEOFF WILLIAMS

Once I decided, it was easy.

My recession came a year earlier than the rest of the country. Early in 2007, I had a slowdown in work. One of my favorite magazine editors decided to leave her job to stay at home with her children, which was great for her family but led to a serious decrease in assignments from the magazine; it also hurt that a two-year project, writing the history of a hospital in Dayton, Ohio, had ended. Writing the history book was a job that meant several serious paychecks from the hospital over the years, until the project came to its natural conclusion.

For whatever reason, I just couldn't find as much work as I had been able to before. But the credit card statements, the ballooning debt from the lending company, my wife's student loans, our ever-increasing health insurance, the mortgage—the bills all kept coming. But somehow, I kept paying everything off. That is, everything except the mortgage.

Almost losing our house woke me up. Getting a letter from the lending company at the end of the year, declaring that I'd better start catching up on payments or risk a lawsuit, gave me a new perspective, too. Every fiber of my being hated the idea of declaring bankruptcy, but I now had about $35,000 of debt, not including back taxes and student loans. I had almost lost my house. It seemed inevitable that we would go through the same thing again.

Selling the house and moving to a smaller one seemed like a possible plan, but our house needed a makeover, including some roofing problems that I couldn't afford to fix. I couldn't imagine who would want to buy our house, and with my credit, I knew that buying another house—even if I sold this one—wouldn't be an easy proposition. But there was more that I kept thinking about. Every dollar I was giving to this company, which was lending me money at 24.5 percent APR, was another dollar I wasn't putting toward our retirement or our daughters' college education.

It's not an easy decision to declare bankruptcy, and I understand and respect why many people drowning in debt don't, and why even many people reading this book, who may be in even more hot water than I was, will think I was wrong to finally call a bankruptcy attorney and make an appointment. But in the end, I decided I had fought the good fight and was empty of any more ammunition. After all, I had extinguished my Roth IRA. I had no savings to speak of. Our house was slowly falling apart. There was nothing else to give my debt. We didn't have a fancy new car to trade in. We didn't have jewelry or expensive electronics. My computer was seven years old. Debt is smothering, because dime by dime, it robs you of your options, and I just didn't feel like I had any more.

Most of all, I thought of our children, who had nothing to do with this but were being affected in subtle ways, if only missing out on things I would have liked to buy them and experiences I wanted to give them, like being able to take piano lessons or having a membership at the YMCA. And certainly they would be affected if we lost our house; and, of course, I kept wondering how I could save for their college education while paying down tens of thousands of dollars in debt. The math was pretty obvious: I couldn't. So I met with an attorney and was soon signing the paperwork. I figured the next few months, as we sorted this out, would be the worst of my life. And it was kind of stressful, but nowhere near what I thought it might be. Emotionally, I felt a huge sense of relief.

Oddly enough, declaring bankruptcy was pretty easy. It was the fifteen years leading up to it that were hard.

CHAPTER TEN

GETTING YOUR GOOD CREDIT BACK AND PREVENTING BAD CREDIT FROM EVER HAPPENING AGAIN

It only takes a few months to get a bad rating,
but it may take years to wipe it clean. It seems a rather
stiff punishment that failing to pay a $10 gas bill
could prevent you from buying a $12,000 home,
but it's true, nevertheless.

CHARLES V. NEAL, JR., A FAMILY FINANCIAL COUNSELOR,
MAKING AN OBSERVATION IN A 1958 NEWSPAPER COLUMN
(AND, NO, THE $12,000 HOUSE IS NOT A TYPO.)

SURE, THIS BOOK IS ABOUT LIVING well with bad credit, but we're not saying you should try to live with it forever. The Land of Bad Credit (LBC) should be no more than a temporary stop on the way to a better place. Think of it as a twelve-hour layover in Cleveland on your way to Maui. (Just teasing you, Cleveland. Chris spent years living in Ohio, and Geoff was born and bred in the Buckeye State, after all.) We're just saying that since you're in the

LBC right now and you've got some time to kill, you might as well make the best of it. But, yes, let's try to get back on the plane as soon as we can.

We said early on in these pages that we weren't going to give you a formula for success, but every self-help book has one, and suddenly we can't resist. If you want to get your good credit back, here are two simple steps: (1) Pay your bills on time and (2) Don't spend more than you have.

> **Chris:** Oh, so that's *all* there is to it? *(Note sarcasm.)*
>
> **Geoff:** We're saying the steps are simple; I'm not saying they're easy.

For those who have plenty of dough rolling in, it can actually be pretty easy. For those who don't, not so much. But ultimately, that's what you have to do—pay on time and live within your means. One of the benefits of having bad credit—really, really, really bad credit—is that it can *force* you to live within your means because loans and credit lines aren't accessible to you. And if you can train yourself to live completely within your means, then you're going to find your credit score going up. Then when you do have to take out a loan for a house, a car, or something else that's important, you can get the low-interest rates, and low-interest rates will help you to continue living within your means.

Here are a couple of ways you can speed up the process of getting your good credit back, and why we implore you to use caution.

HIRE A COMPANY TO CLEAN UP YOUR CREDIT FOR YOU

Yes, a professional firm really can help. Some of the more respected companies out there include Lexington Law, a consumer advocacy law firm. They are not, as their website states, a credit repair firm. (We're not endorsing Lexington; nor are we saying you should steer clear.) What Lexington does is comb through your credit reports, and with your help, they look for errors. Then you say "go," and they attack with letters and phone calls to clean up your credit report.

If there are no errors, there's not much they can do. They can't fix your credit history. So if you bought a $13,000 car and had it repossessed, neither Lexington Law nor any credit repair company can wave a magic wand and make it go away (no matter what some companies might say).

If you have bad credit, but you're wealthy—by the way, it's very common for an executive making $300,000 a year to have lousy credit—you may find paying for these services appealing. But if you're not swimming in cash, due to drowning in debt, just remember that you can do what any of these credit repair services can do. Instead of money, you just have to be willing to spend the time.

CLEAN UP YOUR CREDIT YOURSELF

Now we endorse *this* idea wholeheartedly. As soon as you have the time and energy, go ahead and try to clean up your credit history on your own. It's not hard, it's just time-consuming. This can be a painstaking task of digging through old piles of records, finding receipts, photocopying, letter writing, e-mails, and phone calls. Many

What Is and Isn't Factored in when Determining Your Credit Score

According to information collected from the website Credit Cards.com, what isn't factored in is your gender, marital status, race, religion, where you were born, or even whether you receive public assistance. Here is what makes up your credit score:

How much you owe (30 percent)
Length of credit history (15 percent)
New credit (10 percent)
Your payment history (35 percent)
Other factors (10 percent)

For example, if you have a diversity of types of loans, like one mortgage, one credit card, and one auto loan, that won't be very troubling to a lender. But if you have eight department store credit cards, your score may take a hit.

people won't have the patience for it. So here's the good news: you don't have to clean it up. Eventually, even if it takes seven or ten years, what's on your credit history will disappear. What's also important to remember—and this is why we're of the mind that you don't need to spend hour after hour cleaning up your record—is that the older the debt, the less important in the lender's mind. What's vital is your recent history. Are you paying things down now? The fact that you blew it five years ago with a bankruptcy or foreclosure isn't going to matter that much if your recent credit history is spotless.

So you can participate in a lot of mental gymnastics and spend hours on paperwork, chasing down bureaucrats at the three major credit bureaus, or you can just watch your credit score go up by following our two-step formula. Pay your bills on time and don't spend more than you have. If you spend more than you have, it's harder to pay your bills on time. And if you spend more than you have—as in taking out more credit card loans or lines of credit—then you won't see your score go up. Pretty elementary stuff, really, and yet, the execution is a lot harder than it looks.

The first step in cleaning up your credit is to ask for your free credit report from the three credit bureaus (Experian, TransUnion, and Equifax), except you can't actually ask them. A little confusing, but what you need to do is go to AnnualCreditReport.com, or call 1-877-322-8228, and get the form (there's one at the website), then fill it out to make your request.

You're entitled to one free report from them every year. So if you really want to be thorough, you can request them all at once, or you may want to stagger your requests every four months, so that you can constantly be getting a read on your situation. Either way, examine your report when you get it, and if you see some injustices on your report, then write them and contest what you see. A couple of things to remember, though:

1. When you write, tell your side of the story and offer whatever copies of documents you can to support your claim. If you're really on top of things, send the letter by certified mail.

2. The credit bureau is required by law to investigate the item, unless, according to the Federal Trade Commission's website, "they consider your dispute frivolous."

3. If they determine that they really have made an error, they have to notify the other two bureaus that there's an inaccuracy.

Another quick, free way to get your credit score—not a report, but your score, if you want to monitor your progress as the months go by—is to check out CreditKarma.com. It's a website run by one of the main three credit bureaus, TransUnion, so it's just one piece of the puzzle. It's not an actual FICO score, which is what lenders use to determine if they'll give you a loan. But it will give you a pretty accurate idea of where you are on the credit score ladder. It's free because it is advertiser supported, so if you sign up, you will see a lot of offers for credit cards; mostly, if you have bad credit, they'll be offering you secured credit cards.

Speaking of which . . .

ABOUT SECURED CREDIT CARDS

If you don't know, this is another way of rebuilding your credit. These are kind of like prepaid cards, in that you put your own money in them and then use them like a credit card. The important distinction is that secured credit cards will help you rebuild your credit. Prepaid cards won't. Otherwise, they're virtually alike.

Well, there's a little more to it. With a secured credit card, you're giving them some money as a deposit. Think of it as collateral in case you spend the money on the credit card and never pay it back. So you fork over, say, $300 and then start using it like a regular credit card. There's interest, just like a regular credit card, and you should pay it down every month, just like a regular credit card. There also may be an annual fee, just like a lot of regular credit cards.

It's those fees and the interest rate that you need to be aware of. Some secured credit cards are so loaded down with the fees and high-interest rates that you might as well just take your cash and use it to start a fire in the fireplace—just as useful and kind of fun to watch.

You can find good or bad secured credit cards by checking out credit card comparison sites like CreditCards.com, and there's a lot of useful information at Bankrate.com. Obviously, choose the ones with the lowest fees and interest and the best terms possible. If you can't get a decent secured credit card, take that as a sign that you need to keep improving your credit first.

If you do get a secured credit card, which looks exactly like any other credit card (nobody will be able to look at it and know it's secured), your next step is to keep a low balance. Use it, but pay off the balance right away. If you make your payments on time for a year, which is usually what they request, then generally, if it's a good card, you'll get your deposit back, and you'll be transitioned to an unsecured credit card account. And with that step, you'll be on your way back to the Land of Good Credit (LGC). Welcome home.

Of course, you may wonder, once you do return to the LGC, *how many credit cards should I have?* Well, it's hard to argue with the logic of Rick Staszak, a registered financial consultant (RFC) and certified estate planner (CEP). Suffice it to say that he's an expert in wealth management. He works with Financial Network Investment Corporation, an ING company in Pittsburgh. Rick says, "I'd recommend one card. If you have two cards, then the tendency is to use the two cards, and why use two if you have one, and you're paying it off?"

Or just ignore Mr. Staszak's advice and keep our book handy, so you can consult it again in a few years.

Shudder.

Why I No Longer Stress Over Bills

BY GEOFF WILLIAMS

Over the years, the debt I invited into my life, and that was slowly overtaking my life, began to wear down on my mood. I'm lucky that I had a solid support system, with my parents and brother, whom I could always talk to, and then my wife, and always a network of close friends. It never even occurred to me that I might find comfort from debt by drinking, doing drugs, or gambling. Or maybe I just knew that the last thing I could afford was a vice.

But there were many times over the years when my financial situation ate away at my confidence, morale, and self-esteem. I remember sobbing in my basement office on several occasions, convinced that I'd end up losing our house, our car, and all of our earthly possessions because I was behind in my payments.

I can't do this any longer, I kept thinking. Bill collectors were calling, demanding money that I didn't have. Checks weren't coming in fast enough. I always seemed to be paying everything, from our electric bill to our water bill, at the last minute. I felt like an utter failure.

But what really stands out is a business trip I had to make, a three-hour drive one way, but that meant six hours of gas. Before I left, my wife, Susan, and I got into a heated discussion—about money, *of course*—and I stormed out of the house furious, with my nerves completely shot.

I was driving to a gorgeous bed-and-breakfast that overlooked the Ohio River, to review it for a magazine that was paying me to stay there. That happy fact was completely lost on me. Instead, I kept thinking how nice it would be if an oncoming truck swerved into my lane.

But in spite of myself, I wound up having a wonderful time hanging out and meeting the owners of the bed-and-breakfast, having the place mostly to myself, and visiting their little town. Driving back the next day, I sang along with the radio and couldn't believe I had been so upset. Then later, when I saw my wife, and especially our innocent and adorable one-year-old daughter, and remembered my dark thoughts, I was utterly ashamed.

Granted, they were only thoughts, and I never came close to acting on them, but the intensity of those thoughts scared me, and what really gave me pause was suddenly imagining my wife ten years into the future, valiantly trying to give my daughter a good reason why her father had checked out early. There would have been no good reason, of course.

I've never forgotten that trip and how horrible it would have been had I actually done something that stupid. Not that I never get frustrated or depressed by finances now, but I finally have what everyone struggling to pay their bills needs—perspective. Having money is wonderful—no doubt about it. They say money won't buy us happiness, but it still buys a lot of things that will make us happy. But while money helps you *live* your life, you never, ever want to actually confuse it with your *life*.

In fact, of everything I remember about that road trip—and I remember just about every minute—what I can't summon up is exactly what money problems we were having that caused me to be distraught during that road trip. Were we behind on our mortgage? Was it the taxes I wasn't paying since our extra money was going to the credit cards? Something about my wife's student loans? A paycheck that hadn't come? I have no earthly idea. It's both oddly comforting and haunting that something that seemed so important at the time is something that now I can't recall at all. In fact, whenever I think about all the different times I've stressed out over my finances, and I try to remember the specifics, I can't.

LIVING THE GOOD LIFE

The best advice we can give you for living the good life is to realize that you're living a pretty darn good life right now. Sappy as that sounds, one could definitely come to that conclusion after talking with Dan Danford, the CEO of the Family Investment Center, who we mentioned earlier. He makes the astute observation that "many people we assume are wealthy aren't."

Chris: Wait a minute. His name is Dan Danford? Can I call him Dan-Dan?

Geoff: Oh, man, you should go lie down. I think working on this book is starting to take its toll.

Danford concedes that if you're making $34,000 a year, you're going to look at someone making six times that much and assume that person or family is wealthy. But think about it, urges Dan-Dan—er, Danford: "They may be making $200,000 a year, but a lot of people with fancy cars and houses—we look at them, and we assume they're doing great—but many of them are living on credit, and many of them are one paycheck from being bankrupt."

One way we often get into hot water, adds Danford, is that we tend to look at how others are spending their money, and then we spend accordingly. "I've read research suggesting that most people, if you take their circle of friends [into consideration], all make within 15 percent of each other, and it can be a real problem for some folks if you're on the lower end. For those folks trying to spend up to their friends, that can be a tough issue."

That's just another thing to think about, if you're not sure how you got here. Figuring that out, if you haven't already, is critical, because while our two-step formula for getting your good credit back is technically all you need, we could add a third step.

1. Pay your bills on time.

2. Don't spend more than you have.

3. However you got your bad credit, don't do it again.

So while you're trying to reclaim your reputation with lenders, keep asking yourself the question we asked at the beginning of this book—how did you get here? It matters, if you're going to get out, and especially if you're going to follow our fourth step—

Chris: You don't think anyone will think we're making up this formula as we go along?

Geoff: Sssh!

—and that's step number 4: save money for the future.

We know that's difficult. It can be really maddening, and even feel condescending, listening to a wealthy personal finance guru on TV cheerfully tell you and the rest of the audience to "pay yourself first," when you know the credit card company doesn't really see it that way, and if you told your utility company that you're going to pay yourself first, they would likely reply, "Have fun counting your money in the dark." We know this because, as you know, 50 percent of the authors of this book have been through bankruptcy and bad credit. And 100 percent of the authors of this book have struggled with money. We're not wealthy pitchmen speaking down to the masses; we're right there with you, the readers of this book.

But those personal financial gurus are right. One way or another, no matter how impossible it seems today, you've got to strive for the day when you can routinely sock money away for your retirement and for emergencies—and, of course, the day when you'll have good credit, so that if you need to replace your car, want to buy a new home, or simply live your life, you can. If you don't work toward that day, odds are some issue is going to crop up, some expensive issue, and if you aren't prepared for it, you may continue this cycle of struggling with money and credit indefinitely.

There's no reason for that, though. As the old saying goes, it's a nice place to visit, but you wouldn't want to live there. Well, that's how we feel about what we keep calling the Land of Bad Credit. Really, living here isn't so bad—if you have a decent money supply and it's just the low credit score you're living with. Bad credit is a state of mind as much as a situation, and both can change for the better. You can get back to where you used to be, or where you've always wanted to go. It may take time, and if the money gods aren't being kind, it may take some adjusting or sacrifice, but you owe it to yourself to try.

And why do we say you owe it to yourself? Well, in keeping with our money theme, that's easy: You're worth it.

INDEX

ABOUT THE AUTHORS

MOST OF **CHRIS BALISH**'S WORK has been in television, as a producer (Discovery Channel, American Movie Classics), host (the CW Network), journalist (anchoring the local news in Cincinnati and St. Louis) and on-air cable news contributor (MSNBC and CNN), picking up seven local Emmys in the process. But he is also the author of a book particularly well regarded among the environmental community, *How to Live Well Without Owning a Car: Save Money, Breathe Easier and Get More Mileage Out of Life.* He lives in Los Angeles.

GEOFF WILLIAMS CONTRIBUTES REGULARLY to AOL's personal finance blog, WalletPop, and has written for a variety of publications including CNN.com, Bankrate.com, CreditCards.com and *Consumer Reports.* He is also a general interest writer, having seen his stories in numerous magazines from *LIFE* to *Entertainment Weekly* and is the author of the madcap nonfiction narrative, *C.C. Pyle's Amazing Foot Race: The True Story of the 1928 Coast-to-Coast Run Across America.* He lives in Loveland, Ohio, with his wife, Susan and their two daughters, Isabelle and Lorelei.